MW00830109

EMMA STRATTON

# MAKE IT

# How to Write Simple Tech Messaging That Wins Hearts, Minds & Markets

**PAGE TWO**

Cataloguing in publication information
is available from Library and Archives Canada.
ISBN 978-1-77458-408-8 (paperback)
ISBN 978-1-77458-409-5 (ebook)

Page Two
pagetwo.com

Edited by Marni Seneker
Copyedited by Indu Singh
Proofread by Alison Strobel
Cover, interior design, and illustrations by Fiona Lee

punchy.co

*For Tom,*
*my partner in everything.*

# CONTENTS

## PART THREE *IMPLEMENTATION*

# *INTRODUCTION*

**B**ACK IN **2015**, when I decided to launch a consultancy that focused solely on messaging for B2B tech companies, a few folks told me it was a bad idea.

"Startups don't care about words, they only care about their tech," warned a veteran CEO. "It would be safer to start a normal branding agency."

While there was some truth in their advice, I chose to ignore it anyway. Because I'd seen a big problem in B2B tech marketing that needed to be solved: people were struggling to communicate the value of their software.

This problem found me unexpectedly after I left the glossy world of consumer branding to be the head of copy at a B2B marketing agency. I was used to writing punchy copy that made consumers feel an emotional connection to household products like deodorant, tea bags, shampoo—even sex toys. But as a new mom in need of a shorter commute to work, I'd taken this local job on the (naive) assumption that B2B was essentially like B2C. Sure, the products would be different, but I'd still be marketing to people... right?

The messaging document I had to read for my new client, a data management software company, on my first day said otherwise. It was a seven-page doozie packed with technical mouthfuls, like "*We have fully integrated deduplication into our unified data management solution to provide best-in-class performance to dramatically reduce time-to-backup.*" The writing sounded like it was for a robot, not a human.

When I checked out their competitors' websites, I realized every other company talked this way too. Paragraphs and paragraphs of tech-speak, punctuated with headlines bragging about features, market leadership, and innovation. Lots of talk about best-in-class solutions, but no real clue as to what those solutions could actually do for people. In fact, there was hardly a trace of the buyer in any of it.

My first thought was: *If B2B customers like this stuff then they're nothing like B2C customers—in fact, they might not even be entirely human!*

Quickly followed by: *Sh\*t—I might need to find a new job.*

Then I met the company's chief marketing officer the next day, who quickly confessed that messaging was their number one problem. He told me that they couldn't figure out how to communicate the power of their unique platform to buyers. As a result, their marketing performance was spotty at best. Their salespeople were resorting to their own pitches—some better than others—and they were at risk of losing hard-won market share to their competitors.

"We need our messaging to be as good as our technology," he said. "Can you help us?"

I felt relief because my first instincts were right. Buyers weren't connecting with the messaging because it had nothing to do with them—it was all about the platform.

I knew we needed to go beyond the tech to connect with their buyers on a human level. In my B2C days, I learned that forming a connection with consumers was the best way to sell packaged goods like shampoo, snacks, and cleaning products. Why couldn't that work for software, too?

So, we highlighted their buyer's needs and wants in simple, plain language. We illustrated how their situation could change for the better and kept the message focused on the most important things to the buyer, and not simply on all the things about the platform.

The unique value of the client's platform finally became clear, and as a result their marketing campaigns performed better. Salespeople told the same story and sales increased the next quarter.

Since then, it has been my mission to help people communicate the awesomeness of their technology with punchy messaging. I've worked with hundreds of tech companies of every shape and size, from VC-backed startups to household name companies, spanning different industries and technologies. And I've seen firsthand how punchy messaging improves marketing performance, builds a winning perception, and grows market share.

## Messaging Builds the Perception of Your Product

Messaging is how you convey the awesomeness of your product in a succinct way, and is the foundation for consistent sales and marketing activities. It's as simple as that.

Messaging creates an impression of your product, just like an outfit creates an impression of the person wearing

# Messaging is a powerful tool that's available to us all

it. For example, if you saw someone walk by in a power suit and expensive shoes, you'd assume they were successful. But if the same individual walked by in saggy sweatpants and scuffed flip-flops, you'd likely think the opposite. Because the person is a total stranger, their outfit is the only information you have to go on.

The same thing happens when a buyer comes across your product for the first time. Your messaging is all they have to go on, so they make an assumption based on what they read. If your messaging is dense and complicated, people will assume that your product is as well—even if it's one of the most user-friendly solutions on the market! But if your messaging is simply focused on your buyer's needs and wants—and speaks to them like one human to another human—they'll feel like your solution is for them.

Depending on your messaging, that perception could be a major advantage over competitors, or an obstacle in your path to growth.

Years ago, I was chatting with the head of marketing at a sales tech startup. The company had one of the most innovative platforms on the market. Analysts agreed it was the best. However, their messaging was costing them sales. It dove into the technical weeds of what made their technology so good, which resulted in scientific language that was hard to digest. Buyers showed up to sales calls with the assumption that the platform was "more than what they needed" or "a little too advanced"—perceptions that salespeople had to work against constantly.

On the other hand, their direct competitor, who sold an inferior product, was quickly gaining market share with simple messaging. Instead of focusing on sophisticated technical features, the competitor highlighted what people could do with the product and made the value clear, simple, and relatable. In comparison, they looked like the friendlier, easier-to-use option. As a result, people bought the competitor's product, even though it offered far fewer features and less functionality.

Messaging is a powerful tool that's available to us all—and there's a way to learn how to do it well. But first, let's get clear on where it fits in the big picture of your marketing.

## Where Messaging Fits in the Marketing Landscape

Messaging is often used synonymously with other things like storytelling, copywriting, and even positioning. But messaging has its own distinct and rightful place in the marketing world: after positioning and before copywriting and other content creation.

Messaging is one of the first ways you bring positioning to life. Positioning, as described by the expert April Dunford in her book *Obviously Awesome*, "is the act of deliberately defining how [your product is] the best at something a defined market cares a lot about." It clarifies where your product fits in the market, who it's for, and the unique value it offers. Your positioning strategy guides messaging development.

Messaging is what you say to help your buyer grasp why your product matters. It translates your positioning into key messages that describe how your product or company delivers that unique value. Messaging becomes the playbook for clear and consistent marketing and sales materials.

After messaging comes copywriting. While messaging is *what* you say about your product, copywriting is *how* you communicate those messages across different channels and mediums. Because you can't just repeat the same handful of messages again and again and again, you have to flex them to inspire your buyer to act across all kinds of instances. Messaging gives copywriters the freedom to be creative with word choice, but provides guardrails to make sure everything adds up to a clear, consistent perception. Without messaging, copywriting could cover anything and everything about your product—creating an unclear or confused perception.

### HOW MESSAGING RELATES TO POSITIONING AND COPYWRITING

**Positioning:** Clarifies what your product is, who it's for, and what it does best

**Messaging:** Articulates how your product delivers unique value and brings positioning to life

**Copywriting:** Communicates messaging across different marketing channels to drive action

In an ideal world, you'll always write messaging with the benefit of a positioning exercise that came beforehand, and your messaging will be handed off to copywriters who can creatively apply the messaging. But let's face it—we rarely have the luxury of working in the ideal state! High-growth companies don't always have the time or resources to do all three distinct steps. Sometimes, you've only got time to do the copywriting on a landing page or do the messaging without the benefit of clear positioning in place.

That's why this book gives you a practical, broader approach to messaging that includes the strategic thinking of positioning as well as some of the wordsmithing that happens in copywriting. So, no matter what the circumstances are, you're covered.

## How to Follow the Punchy Messaging Process in This Book

While consulting with tech companies over the years, I realized there was no standard best practice for messaging—and this was making life harder for a lot of founders, marketers, and leadership teams.

Developing messaging for technology products is complex, and it can feel challenging (even paralyzing) when you don't have a proven process to follow. That's why I created a step-by-step process to help you write messaging that resonates with your customers, so you can drive growth in the market; it works for anything you need to write messaging for, from a small product release to a billion-dollar company.

This book is broken down into three parts to make it easier for you to tackle one step at a time: strategy, writing, and implementation.

In strategy, you will learn how to set your focus for messaging. You'll identify the right buyer, understand what truly motivates them, and connect them to your product's best qualities. You'll learn how to stand out in the market by highlighting your product's unique value.

Next, you'll start writing with my favorite formulas to conquer the blank page, so you can get to a good working draft of messaging faster and with confidence. Then you'll learn simple ways to edit your value proposition and benefits until they're as punchy as can be.

Finally, you will learn how to implement new messaging and get it out into the world. In this final section we will also explore how to scale messaging internally by bringing others into the messaging process, and when it's appropriate to do so.

My goal is to give you little techniques that create big results, so you build confidence in your abilities. Trust me when I say you already have everything it takes to write punchy messaging.

Let's do this!

# PART ONE

# STRATEGY

Find the right angle for your messaging. In this section,
you'll dig into your customers' pains and desires
and map them to your product's best features—laying
the foundation for messaging that resonates.

# 1

## MESSAGE FOR THEM (NOT YOU)

Put your customer first

**M**ESSAGING IS more than just words; it's nailing down the essence of what makes your technology so great. With just a handful of sentences, messaging translates a complex product into new possibilities that your buyers will happily open their wallets for.

Messaging has always been important, but now it's more critical than ever. Your market is noisy, with a new competitor popping up every other day. Every company is claiming that they're number one. It's not enough to have the best product anymore. You have to be the best at showing buyers how your product could fit into their life and make it better—as quickly as possible.

You have to make it punchy.

The *Cambridge Dictionary* defines "punchy" as "expressing something effectively and with power, often using fewer and shorter words"—and it's the key to standing out in the market and connecting with your buyers.

Customers are out there looking for products and companies they can trust. Ones that understand their challenges and have real solutions for them. And they have to search them out in a sea of big claims and complicated tech talk—while juggling everything else in their day-to-day. It's not easy for buyers these days.

Punchy messaging is like a bright red life preserver in that sea of noise, signaling a way out of that mess. It stands out by addressing the customers' most urgent needs and draws them toward the relief of your product's solution.

## Inside-Out versus Outside-In Messaging

One of the first startups I worked with was a biotech company founded by a trio of machine-learning prodigies. They'd built an impressive platform that analyzed digital images of specimens from pathology labs, and needed new messaging to go to market.

The chief technology officer (CTO) was drawing pictures on the whiteboard to show me how their machine-learning models worked. There were lots of frantic squiggles, numbers, and arrows. And even more talk of "cloud storage" and "big data analytics"—two features that made the software so good under the hood. (In their defense, it was 2013 and pretty much every B2B software company was jamming "cloud" into their messaging.)

But this wasn't what clinics and pathologists got excited about—or even understood. They had been living without cloud storage for decades and felt they would continue to do so for the foreseeable future. Hence the need for messaging work.

Then it was my turn at the whiteboard. I told them that instead of explaining the tech, we needed to translate what it could mean to their buyers. So I asked them: Why was cloud storage so important? What new things did it help their buyers do? How could it change their routine? And why did that even matter?

After some back-and-forth, I started to understand why these two features were so important.

"Cloud storage" meant that doctors around the world could collaborate to make better cancer diagnoses and treatment plans—waaaay faster than ever before. And "big data analytics" meant their platform could detect cancers in digital images that the human eye couldn't see on a slide under a microscope.

I flopped back in my chair with surprise. This startup was *literally* helping to cure cancer. (How many people can actually say that?!) And yet, it had taken forty-five minutes of technical doodling and conversation to figure that out from the features.

The magic of their platform—this new ability to change the way people were diagnosing cancer—was being completely buried in the technical weeds. The founders were stuck in the minutiae of how it worked and talked about their product from mainly that perspective. They led with what was on the inside of their platform.

But the rest of the world—their buyers included—saw their platform from the completely opposite perspective. They were on the outside looking in on a new technology. And they needed a better reason than "big data analytics" to drive them to learn more.

## Punchy Messaging Goes Outside In, Not Inside Out

You know your product's awesomeness stems from key features. But leading with them in your messaging doesn't capture the awesomeness in your buyers' eyes, because it's not clear how those features might help them.

An inside-out message—for example, "unleash self-service data analytics"—puts the burden on the reader to figure out what that means, where it could fit in their daily routine, and what problems it might solve. That's too much work for a busy buyer.

Punchy messaging makes it easier for buyers by aligning with their perspective and going from the outside in—leading with the value to your buyer. For example, the outside-in version of the previous example would be "now you can spot patterns, interpret trends, and answer key questions with your data." It translates what the feature means to them in the context of their daily life.

Messaging isn't really about your product—it's about the cool new things your buyer will be able to do, be, and feel, thanks to your product. Those are what people are *really* buying, and that's the true awesomeness of your product.

If you've been approaching messaging from an inside perspective, there's no shame in it; inside out is the norm for many companies. Marketers, builders, and technical founders are all living on the inside of their products, so it's no wonder that their thinking naturally orients from an inside-out perspective.

But when you make a mindset shift of leading with what matters to your customer, your messaging gets stronger. You can do that by following the VBF rule, which sits at the heart of punchy messaging.

In VBF, "V" is for value proposition, "B" is for benefit, and "F" is for feature—these are the core ingredients of messaging. Before we go any further, let's nail down their definitions once and for all, because the line often blurs between them. While they're closely related, each has a different job to do in messaging.

Here's a handy way of looking at them with a little help from *Star Wars*.

## A Feature Is like a Secret Weapon

A feature (also feature sets) is something special your product has or can do. Think of it like a secret weapon inside your product that makes it powerful. Examples of features are "real-time analytics," "custom dashboard," and "anomaly detection."

In *Star Wars*, the Force is like a feature. It's a powerful energy field that binds the galaxy together. And if you know *Star Wars*, then you know it's a big deal. But if you haven't seen the movies, my explanation of the Force is massively underselling it.

That's what happens when you just explain a feature—people don't get why it's so great. Unless you get into the benefits.

## A Benefit Is like a Superpower

A benefit is something new your customer can do, be, or feel, thanks to a feature. Think of it like a new superpower they get when they use your product. Benefits commonly speak to an individual's needs and bring to life the power of features. Examples of benefits are "get an instant view across your financials," "reduce manual work and errors," and "speed up the application process for candidates."

In *Star Wars*, the Force gives Luke Skywalker all kinds of wonderful superpowers. He can do backflips with a lightsaber. He can fly a spaceship through a crevice with his eyes shut. He can even control people's minds!

These are all benefits of the Force—cool new things Luke can do, be, and feel. Now, anyone can clearly see how powerful the Force is. Aren't they way more interesting than my energy field explanation?!

## A Value Proposition Is like a Big Win

A value proposition is how multiple benefits add up to a bigger goal your customer is hoping to achieve. Value propositions often connect to larger business goals, or big aspirations. The benefit of "having an instant view across financials" could lead to a value proposition of a business being able to "fuel more growth opportunities with better cash flow."

In *Star Wars*, Luke Skywalker has a goal of defeating Darth Vader and bringing peace to the galaxy. All the fancy backflips and lightsaber antics the Force enables are in service to this bigger, more meaningful goal.

Value propositions are how you connect the dots between a feature and meaningful business value, which is a must when you're selling an expensive B2B product. If Luke had to get sign-off from his boss to buy the Force, he couldn't just talk about the backflips he'd be able to do— he'd have to connect it to a broader goal like defeating the Empire. And that's why we have value propositions.

Benefits and value propositions are how you translate features into things that buyers understand and want. We need all three, but they have to come in the right order.

## Go Outside In with the VBF Rule

Structure messaging that champions your customers by following the VBF Rule. The letters V-B-F appear in the same order you want to use in your messaging: lead with value, benefit comes second, and the feature is last. VBF hooks your buyers' interest by leading with a desirable outcome, then draws them into the details of what they'll be able to do with it. The *how* of it all—the features—take a humble back seat.

Outside of B2B tech, VBF makes obvious sense. Let's say we have a fancy blender that features commercial-grade blades. The benefit of the blades is the ability to make vitamin-packed smoothies in a snap. And that results in the value proposition of eating healthier every day.

Look at the difference between leading with the value in VBF and leading with the feature. Which do you think is more compelling?

*Example: Fancy Blender*

| VBF (Outside In) | FBV (Inside Out) |
|---|---|
| **Eat healthier every day** | **Commercial-grade blades** |
| Make vitamin-packed smoothies in a snap with commercial-grade blades. | Our commercial-grade blades make vitamin-packed smoothies quickly, so you can eat healthier. |

When you put them side by side, it's easy to see which one is more compelling. The VBF version champions the customer by showing the cool new thing you can do with the blender. In contrast, the FBV version champions the product by leading with the cool new thing the fancy blades can do.

The VBF version speaks to you on a human level. You can relate to the desire to eat healthier, and you want to do it with a great-tasting smoothie that takes minimal effort to make. To me (assuming I'm the target consumer), the VBF message shows me how I could be a better version of myself, thanks to those commercial-grade blades.

Now let's see VBF in the context of B2B tech—for observability software that engineers use to monitor the performance of all their applications. The feature is a dashboard that delivers the benefit of seeing your entire tech stack's performance, which leads to the value of being able to resolve issues with systems and applications before they have an impact on your end customers.

*Example: Observability Software*

| VBF (Outside In) | FBV (Inside Out) |
|---|---|
| **Resolve issues before customers notice** | **Intuitive dashboard** |
| Stop problems before they start by monitoring your entire stack's performance in one dashboard. | Our dashboard provides visibility into your entire stack's performance, so you can resolve issues before customers notice. |

Which headline is more compelling and likely to keep you reading? If you're just skimming the headline (like pretty much everyone does online), the VBF version leads with a powerful outcome for the buyer, while the other is just describing a dashboard.

# Punchy messaging connects with your buyer on a human level

The VBF version illustrates how a dashboard empowers someone to do great things and acknowledges that software is a tool for humans to use—not the other way round. It respects your buyer's needs and abilities by making your customer the hero, and your product the sidekick.

## Simple Is Memorable

Punchy messaging connects with your buyer on a human level and leads with what matters to them. But you have to marry that with simplicity to effectively communicate it to buyers and build a consistent perception in your market.

Few tech CEOs are famous for their clothing choices like Steve Jobs. For years, he showed up to work in the same outfit of black turtleneck, blue jeans, and New Balance sneakers. (I dare you to picture Steve Jobs without that black turtleneck peeping below his serious chin.) Three simple items, worn every day, created the perception of a man too busy with big decisions to bother with wardrobe variety like the rest of us—and he became famous for it.

Now, imagine if Jobs had a typical wardrobe stuffed with all kinds of things: random T-shirts, button-up shirts, formal trousers, hoodies, Nikes, etc. He would have thrown on a different outfit every day, some better than others, with none of it adding up to a clear style. I doubt anyone would remember his look. His minimalist three-piece wardrobe was far more effective in conveying a single-minded, memorable style.

The same applies to your messaging. You want to keep it simple, so people can easily repeat it again and again until you become known for it in the market. Your messaging gets used by all kinds of people—colleagues, partners, and external agencies—and if there are too many different things to choose from, like a crowded closet, people will end up putting together their own looks. And it won't add up to a clear, consistent, and memorable point of view.

The fewer options in your messaging, the more effective it will be. To make it punchy, we're going to take a minimalist approach to messaging that follows VBF. You'll lead with one value proposition, followed by three benefits that are delivered by your product's best features. This structure will make it easier for you to communicate the awesomeness of your product (or anything else you need to message) to buyers in a simple way.

| VALUE PROPOSITION | | |
| --- | --- | --- |
| BENEFIT 1 | BENEFIT 2 | BENEFIT 3 |
| FEATURES | FEATURES | FEATURES |

Over the course of this book, you'll be working toward filling out this messaging framework to translate your product into outcomes your buyer cares about.

And it all starts with your customer.

# FOCUS ON THE ONE

## Identify your A+ customer

2

**B**Y NOW YOU know that messaging opens the door to your product and tells your buyers why they should walk through it. The better you know your buyers, the more likely they'll want to walk through that open door.

Years ago, I went to a lame holiday party at the company I worked for that featured a white elephant gift exchange. If you've never heard of this gift-giving tradition before, it's where everyone brings in a wrapped present and puts it in a big pile under a tree (or, in our case, on a spare desk). Then everyone pulls a number from a hat, which dictates your place in line to choose a random gift, open it in front of everybody, and pretend you don't hate it.

I remember that Jeff, the rumpled IT guy, unwrapped a pack of fruity-flavored lip glosses. Caroline, who didn't drink, was the proud owner of a beer koozie shaped like a fish. And I got a huge box of coconut-covered chocolates, which is the only form of chocolate I don't like. You can tell the game was created over a hundred years ago when people had fewer gift options and lower expectations. Because it doesn't work anymore.

You can't choose the right gift for a mystery person because you have no clue what they want. Just like you can't expect to create the right messaging for a mystery buyer. If you don't know who they are, every sentence you write is a shot in the dark.

That's why you have to get clear on who you're actually writing for before you start writing.

## Write for One Person to Resonate with a Crowd

Figuring out who you're talking to in B2B tech isn't straight-forward. You're likely dealing with multiple audiences, personas, and stakeholders in the sales cycle. And ambitious growth goals often throw even *more* people into the mix. This brings up the very natural urge to try to speak to everyone in your messaging, to find the elusive "one message that will rule them all" that will take care of this complex audience problem.

Unfortunately, this mythical message doesn't exist. Every audience has their own challenges, needs, and wants. When you try to cover them all in one message, you strip out these important details in the quest to appeal to everyone. And when you try to appeal to everyone inside an organization, your messaging ends up sounding like it's written for a corporate entity.

But businesses don't read your messaging—people do. While your company targets other businesses, your messaging will be read by the people *inside* those businesses. If you want to make the awesomeness of your product stand out, you must decide who you're writing for—even if you want to sell your product to multiple audiences. Then you can write messaging that speaks their language, so your solution feels like it's made uniquely for them.

The effect is like a dog whistle, which makes a high-frequency sound that humans can't hear. If you blew one at a park, people around you wouldn't notice anything. But every dog would have their ears pricked to attention because they heard that whistle loud and clear. Similarly, when you write for one specific buyer, your messaging stands out and gets their attention. It draws them in by speaking about what matters to them. And person by person, you effectively reach a larger crowd than you'd ever reach with a generic message.

You do this by focusing on not just any customer, but your A+ customer. Your A+ customer is a raving fan of your product. They love it so much that they refer your product to others without being asked.

Identifying your A+ customer is where positioning and messaging rub elbows. If you've already gone through a formal positioning process, then your A+ customer is the target audience you've defined. And if you don't have the time to do a full positioning exercise, finding your A+ customer will help you make up for it. This exercise can be easy or challenging, depending on your company. If you're a startup with a single product and a clear use case, your A+ customer might be clear to you—for example, a social media scheduler might have an A+ customer in a busy solopreneur. If you're selling a larger platform or multiple products to enterprises, it can be more difficult to understand who you're talking to in that group.

## How to Identify Your A+ Customer

Your A+ customer is likely hiding in plain sight among a lot of C- customers. These are some of my favorite questions to sniff them out.

- **Who are your happiest customers?** Sometimes this is the only question you have to ask. Look for the types of customers who love your product and often refer it to others. Who churns less and renews more?

- **Who gets the most value from your product?** Your product solves lots of problems, but some are worth paying more for. Which customers see your product as a must-have? Who needs your product the most?

- **Who are the super users of your product?** A+ customers tend to be aligned with your product vision, so look for customers who are using more sophisticated features and influencing your roadmap.

For example, I worked with a cash flow management platform that had been steadily growing for five years by selling to heads of finance at all kinds of companies: global enterprises, multinational businesses, and high-growth companies. They were different audiences with different needs, so the startup wasn't sure what to talk about in their new company messaging. They had lots of customers, but not all of them were A+ customers. In fact, quite a few of them were C- customers: traditional multinational businesses that were hard to sell to, thought the platform was too expensive, and only used the basic features.

Their A+ customers were the opposite: private equity–backed, high-growth companies that needed advanced control over their cash flow. The platform's value was clear to them, so the deals moved faster and they signed without balking at price. To target these customers we tailored the messaging for the finance lead in this type of business, focusing on their specific needs and wants around speed and control.

At first, the team worried about favoring one customer at the expense of others. Sure, the traditional corporations were C- customers, but revenue was revenue, right? Their fear of narrowing in on one type of customer wasn't unique—almost every company I've consulted with has grappled with this. Speaking to *fewer* people feels at odds with selling to *more* customers. But here's the paradox— focusing on your A+ customers doesn't automatically slam the door shut on other types of customers. It has a halo effect that extends to other like-minded buyers.

By focusing on the messaging that cool, high-growth companies cared about, my client attracted other like-minded people who wanted that too. They began to attract and sign multinational businesses that aspired to be like their high-growth A+ customers, none of which would have happened if they'd just thrown one generic message at everyone.

## What If I Have Different Audiences?

Even if your product serves multiple audiences and job titles, you want to focus on one A+ customer in your messaging.

If you're an early-stage startup, this is critical to gain traction through your marketing. By doubling down on

You must decide who you're writing for—**even if you want to sell to multiple audiences**

one customer type, you become the obvious choice for them—leading to more sales. As you grow, you can eventually expand beyond that. So even if you want to attract two audiences, focus on the one that best represents your A+ customer to support your growth goals.

If you're at a larger company juggling lots of audiences, you can write separate messaging for each one. But if you need top-level messaging that sits above all audiences, you still want to focus on the A+ customer. This becomes a balancing act of appealing to the best customers without alienating the rest.

## Is My A+ Customer the User, the Buyer, or the Decision-Maker?

Even in a buying group, you want to angle your messaging toward the A+ customer. There are typically six to ten people in a B2B buying group—even with buyers, users, influencers, and decision-makers, you still have to pick a person to focus on.

So ask yourself who you're *really* talking to.

You might think the A+ customer is the person with the most clout in the buying group, like the chief information officer (CIO) who signs off on the deal, or the head of IT who has final veto power over solutions. But just because the CEO or CTO (or some other C-suite person) is in your buying group, doesn't mean your messaging should totally focus on them. Because chances are they're not the ones hunting around for solutions, or the ones who will ultimately use them. They're probably relying on colleagues to make recommendations.

In many cases, your A+ customer is the champion of the group—the person who's motivated to push the solution through. They're the ones doing the legwork of researching options and reading your messaging. Remember that messaging is the door opener to your product and invites people to take the next step forward, whether that's requesting a demo or contacting sales. There are other places to serve up information for other people throughout the buying cycle.

## What If I'm Trying to Reach a Different Customer Than Who We Sell to Today?

Sometimes, your company is at a point where your A+ customers aren't enough to support your growth target. You have to change strategy and appeal to a new audience. But this can be a tricky balancing act as you try to reach a new crowd without losing touch with the old crowd that's keeping the lights on.

Instead of throwing away one customer for another, consider a phased approach where you highlight common ground between the two audiences. For example, I worked with a fintech company whose A+ customers were bootstrapped startup founders. But they wanted to go upmarket and sell to heads of finance of venture-backed startups, too.

These two types of customers still wanted a lot of the same things: access to capital and daily efficiencies. The one key difference was that the heads of finance also cared about scaling finance operations, which was less relevant to the startup founders. To target both customers, we focused on their shared needs and goals in the majority

of the messaging, and addressed the idea of scaling operations within one benefit. This phased approach supported
their expansion into a new audience without alienating
their existing customers.

## What If My Startup Doesn't Have Any Customers Yet?

If it's early days and you don't have an existing pool of customers, make your best guess based on the data you have
in front of you. Ask yourself what kind of customer you'd
gladly have. Who has the problem your product solves?
Who would get the most value out of it? These questions
will help you home in on a potential A+ customer.

The good news is that writing messaging for a defined
customer—even if it's your best guess—will be more effective than writing something for absolutely everyone. It will
give you a truer read on whether it resonates with your
potential target.

## Beware the Curse of Knowledge

Do you know you're living with the Curse of Knowledge?
Don't worry, I have it too.

The Curse of Knowledge is a cognitive bias that happens when you know a lot about a subject. For example,
cooking. You have so much experience stored up in your
brain that you can't remember what it was like to *not* know
all that stuff. You can't help but assume that everyone else
knows what you know too. This leads to writing that's

too advanced for the reader. You dive into the nuances of achieving a fluffy soufflé for an audience that doesn't know how to properly crack an egg.

The Curse of Knowledge is why so much tech messaging goes over people's heads. When you know a lot about your product, your natural tendency will be to write messaging that assumes your reader knows what you know. You unconsciously assume that other people see the inherent value of a feature like you do. That's why you want to get clear on your customer's level of knowledge about your product, so you can meet them where they're at.

Once you've identified your A+ customer, take a minute to consider how much they know about products and solutions like yours. Ask yourself these questions.

### How Tech-Savvy Are They?

There are technical buyers and business buyers, and there's a spectrum of tech-savviness between the two. Get clear on how technical (or not) your A+ customers are so your messaging hits the right note with them. Are they technical folks who are well versed in using and buying software? Or are they new to it all?

### How Aware of Your Solution Are They?

Do they have a good idea what your software does, or is this the first time they're learning about a product like yours? If you're in a mature category—like CRM (customer relationship management), for example—chances are your customer has a strong understanding of your solution and what it does. However, if you're in a new or emerging category, they might not even know a solution like yours exists.

Knowing where your A+ customer is in relation to your tech (and remembering your curse!) will help shape your messaging in later chapters.

‖‖‖‖‖‖‖‖‖‖‖‖‖‖‖‖‖‖‖‖‖‖‖‖‖‖‖‖‖‖‖‖‖‖‖‖‖‖‖‖‖‖‖‖‖‖‖‖‖‖‖‖‖‖‖‖‖‖‖‖‖‖‖‖‖‖‖‖‖‖‖‖‖‖‖‖‖‖‖‖‖‖‖

# A PUNCHY PEP TALK

On the surface, this chapter's task may seem easy, but it can be surprisingly hard to decide and align on an A+ customer. You might not be sure your startup has found one yet. Your colleagues might disagree with each other. Your boss or CEO may insist on selling to absolutely everyone (that one is really tough to deal with).

But don't let that discourage you—it's all part of the process. And the work you put in now will make the entire messaging development process easier, more effective, and more enjoyable.

So, bring people together and have the necessary conversations. Work with the data you have. Trust your instincts. And if you're still not sure, just take your best guess.

‖‖‖‖‖‖‖‖‖‖‖‖‖‖‖‖‖‖‖‖‖‖‖‖‖‖‖‖‖‖‖‖‖‖‖‖‖‖‖‖‖‖‖‖‖‖‖‖‖‖‖‖‖‖‖‖‖‖‖‖‖‖‖‖‖‖‖‖‖‖‖‖‖‖‖‖‖‖‖‖‖‖‖

# FEEL WHAT YOUR BUYER FEELS

## Get real about their pains and desires

**P**UNCHY MESSAGING gets real with people about how they can use your product to either solve a pain or achieve a goal that matters to them. Because right now every potential buyer is thinking, "Eh, who cares?"

I know it's harsh, but it's true. When you're a busy marketer, it's easy to forget the simple truth that nobody cares about your product unless you give them a damn good reason to. Not because your buyers are selfish, uncaring people. They're just too busy thinking about stuff that's going on in their own lives. You and I are no different. We think about issues at work and our personal plans for the future. We think about our problems, big and small, and how they make us feel. We think about the things we wish we had and the things we'd like to change.

There's not a lot of room for your product to muscle its way in there. To get the buyer's attention, you've got to connect the dots between your product and the things they already care about: their pains and desires.

Pains and desires are a motivating force inside your buyer's mind, like a strong river current. It's always there, pushing people to make a change in their situation. When you tap into your buyers' pains and desires, your product benefits from this current and gains traction with them faster. On the flip side, if you just try and get them to care about your latest feature or how it works, you're swimming upstream and fighting the current. That's a lot of work. You could easily tire out (and probably sink to the bottom!).

Tapping into your buyer's pains and desires is key to messaging that resonates. But you have to go beyond the stiff, generic, business-y sounding problem statements that are rife in B2B marketing and connect with people on an authentic, human level.

## Real Talk Cuts Through the Noise

After graduating college with an English degree, I lived in Brooklyn and worked as a lowly publishing assistant, making $28,000 a year. I was essentially broke all the time. Every five-dollar purchase put me at risk of going into overdraft because I never checked my bank account balance to see what I could safely spend. I was too scared to do it. I was afraid to go in there and see that I only had $2.32 to my name, so I avoided it completely and made spending decisions based on my gut (which turned out to be a pretty terrible financial strategy). I was your classic English major who sucked at money. Not long after that, I noticed messaging for a new online bank. And the headline message knocked the wind right out of me: *Take the fear out of checking your account balance.*

It's like the bank was speaking directly to my soul. I'd never told anyone about my banking shame, but here was this company that knew exactly what I'd been thinking. It was wild how this company understood me. I kept reading. And the messaging kept connecting to the pain I felt, like never really knowing what I could afford. It even made a loving joke about English majors and personal finances. (How did this company get into my mind?!)

I felt seen and heard. And the more I read, the more I started to believe the company actually understood me and might have a solution worth exploring. So I opened an account and became a loyal customer for many, many years. And it all started with a message that got real with me and tapped into the undeniable pain I was experiencing.

Now, if this bank had taken a typical B2B approach to messaging, the headline might have said something like "drive better financial decision-making" or "optimize your savings." Most pains and desires you see in B2B messaging are sanitized with dry, corporate language that manages to squeeze all the realness out of it. In an effort to make the messaging sound serious and smart, it just ends up feeling totally unrelatable and unemotional.

## The Power of Being Real with Your Customers

There's a lot of noise in B2B marketing, and buyers have become numb to all the fluff and corporate-speak. This presents an incredible opportunity for your company to stand out by being real in your messaging. Here's what I've seen time and time again with my clients who have taken this approach.

### It Attracts the Right People

In the last chapter, you learned that speaking to one customer is more effective than trying to reach everybody. The online bank's headline wasn't meant for everyone. Accountants and type A people wouldn't connect with the message at all. But for the many creative, disorganized people like me, it was powerfully spot on. I was their target.

### It Makes People Feel Something

You add oomph to your messaging when it makes people feel something. When I read the online bank's message, my mind went straight back to all the times I felt nervous about my personal finances, which made me feel those emotions all over again, fanning the flames of my desire to finally do something about it.

### It Builds Trust on the Page

Being real about what your buyer is facing naturally builds trust with them. It shows that you understand their world and what they're trying to achieve, which honors their lived experience. Because the old days of BS-ing people are over. Customers want honesty and truth about how you can help them. It's not just the right thing to do—it's what people have come to expect.

I worked with a cybersecurity company whose platform offered a remarkably hands-off solution for busy security teams. They were displacing clunky, legacy systems that took a lot of time and effort to maintain. During customer interviews, several users described the pain my client's software solved in the same way. They told me how they were relieved to have found "a system they didn't have to hand-hold or babysit," which allowed them to "finally get their nights and weekends back." They were being real with me about their challenges. So we used this language in their messaging, which later got incorporated onto their homepage—resulting in an increase in demo requests.

Being real starts with identifying the pains and desires that matter the most to your buyer. But how do you find them?

## -✧- GRAB MY INTERVIEW GUIDE -✧-

When you're ready to do some customer interviews, head on over to punchy.co/CustomerInterviewGuide and download my interview guide, which includes my favorite questions that inspire the best answers.

## How to Find Your A+ Customer's Real Pains and Desires

You likely already know a lot about your customer's problems and goals (and, if not, we'll get to that). This exercise will help you explore them on a deeper, more human level. Take a moment to put yourself in your customer's shoes and imagine a typical day in their life. See things from their perspective. Then answer the following questions.

- **What are their smack-in-the-face challenges?** These are the problems that drive your buyer nuts. Think of daily issues that your buyers keep running up against. For example, a workflow breakdown or pointless manual tasks.

- **What wakes them up at 2 a.m. in a cold sweat?** These are the big, existential problems that weigh on your buyer's mind—and often map to larger business-level challenges. For example, needing to attract better talent to their organization.

- **What are their goals on the horizon?** These are your buyer's larger goals and aspirations—things they'd like to achieve. For example, making collaboration easier across multiple departments.

- **What are their deep-down desires?** These point to personal motivations and the things people want for themselves and how they'd like to change for the better. For example, to be more respected in their job.

Look at these questions through both a professional and personal lens—because every "work" problem has a "life" impact too.

## Where to Research Your Buyer's Pains and Desires

If you're not totally familiar with your buyer, you can do some messaging research to understand them better and fill in any blanks. I call it "messaging research" because it's a bit different from market and customer research. Instead of broad insights, messaging research is narrowly focused on your customer's key pains and desires, and how they talk and feel about them (which come into play in the following chapters). It's so helpful to the messaging process that I recommend doing it, even if you do know your buyer pretty well.

# Go beyond
the stiff, generic,
business-y
sounding problem
statements

Here are some of my favorite ways to do messaging research.

**Interview current customers or ideal buyers:** Speaking to your existing A+ customers—or people who represent them—is the best way to understand their pains and desires, in their own words. Customers also have a knack for describing things in way simpler terms than we marketers do. (Between you and me, some of the best messaging I've ever written came directly from a customer quote.) Ask them to describe their pains and desires and record everything, so you can mine it later for messaging gold.

**Ask your sales team:** I'm a huge fan of talking to salespeople because they're the ones chatting with buyers about their problems all day long. And, let's face it, many are doing their own thing messaging-wise and just seeing what works. One good conversation with sales can give you the type of insights you'd get from running both a customer survey *and* a messaging test. It's wildly efficient, which is why I do it in every messaging engagement. (And you should too.) If your sellers aren't available, you can listen to sales call recordings for insights.

**Check out review sites:** If you don't have access to customers, check out what they're saying on peer review sites like G2 and Gartner—it's a quick way to see how customers describe the challenges they're trying to solve. If your product has lots of reviews, you may spot trends in common challenges. If you don't have many reviews, check out similar products that will likely feature similar challenges.

**Review RFPs:** If you sell enterprise software, past RFPs are a treasure trove of information. Your buyer is quite literally listing all the things they're looking for in a solution. I know lots of savvy product marketers who keep all their RFPs for future reference in messaging.

## Say It like You Would at a BBQ

Once you've identified your customer's pains and desires, it's time to get real with them by describing them like your customer would.

As a B2B marketer, it's easy to get into the habit of describing customer problems in robotic language, like "need to improve productivity and eliminate risk" and "correct operational inefficiencies at scale." *Beep-boop-beep.* While these phrases may be technically correct, their vague formality ignores all the emotion and nuance wrapped up inside these problems, which are often the real motivation for people to buy the product.

If your list of pains is looking a bit robotic, try my "say it like you would at a BBQ" exercise. Read each one and ask yourself if that's how your buyer might talk about it to a friend at a BBQ on the weekend. Would they really say "we need to gain operational efficiencies at scale" while drinking a beer? If it's not something they'd likely say in real life, try rewriting it. Think about what the problem looks like through their eyes. How might they describe it in their own words?

What details would they add? Would they get emotional?

This exercise is the fast track to more compelling pains and desires to inform your messaging. It also allows you to play around with new ways of talking about problems and solutions beyond your typical in-the-box language.

I was leading this exercise in a Punchy Training Workshop with the marketing team from a software company that helped homebuilders manage their projects and client relationships. We were brainstorming their customer's pains and a marketer said, "They need to streamline client communications." Which wasn't wrong. But it also wasn't how a homebuilder would describe it.

So, I asked her to imagine how the buyer might say it over a burger and beer at a BBQ. What might he say if he was venting to a friend? It was easy to picture the buyer mildly stressed at a BBQ as his phone blew up with calls from clients checking in about their home's progress or their latest change orders.

These contractors were building people's dream homes, so they had to deal with clients bugging them at all hours and trying to follow up. It was a big drain on their time—and something they really wanted to solve. The marketers could clearly see the homebuilder turning to a friend and saying, "I need to get these constant texts, calls, and emails from my clients under control—it's driving me nuts."

See the difference between "need to streamline communications" and "need to get the constant calls, texts, and emails from clients under control"?

The second one is more emotional and real—it's how people actually think and talk. You can picture it in your mind, which makes the problem easy to grasp. And any contractor feeling overwhelmed by texts and emails from their clients will connect with it.

This exercise was really easy for the marketing team to do because they knew their customers well. And that's the kicker—you can know your customer well and still fall into the trap of emotionless, business-speak problems. I see it again and again in my workshops.

What I've learned is that sometimes we just need to feel like we have permission to be real and say it like it is in our marketing. Well, I give you full permission, my friend!

## Is BBQ Talk Appropriate for People in Serious Industries?

If you're in a buttoned-up industry (e.g., finance or government) or have an ultra-technical buyer, you might be wondering if "say it like you would at a BBQ" is right for you. You might worry that it's not serious enough.

Let me be clear: "Saying it like you would at a BBQ" isn't about being unprofessional or inappropriate (or using slang or idioms in your writing). It's an exercise to get more specific about customer problems by using the right words to describe them and acknowledging emotions that go with them.

Over the course of hundreds of messaging engagements, I've interviewed over a thousand customers in very serious jobs like security, IT, and engineering, and I can honestly say they're every bit as human as you and me. I remember talking to a site reliability engineer in relation to an observability platform. The biggest problems he talked about? The sheer panic of getting a system alert in the middle of the night, and how often he ends up missing his son's soccer games on the weekends because of work.

Remember how every work problem has a life impact? This is a prime example—these days, work bleeds into life and vice versa. Every buyer has feelings and a life outside of work that impacts purchasing decisions. So why ignore them?

*Example: Say It like You Would at a BBQ*

| Un-BBQ-Friendly | BBQ-Friendly |
|---|---|
| "Boost developer productivity and retention." | "Keep developers happy by letting them focus on building cool sh*t instead of boring manual tasks." |
| "Eliminate the need for multiple tools." | "Take away the frustration of having to log in to multiple tools every day." |
| "Foster continuous engagement among team members." | "Keep everyone on the team involved." |

## Highlight Their Most Urgent Pains and Desires

Once you have your list of BBQ-friendly pains and desires, you're ready to zero in on the ones that matter most to your buyer. Because not all pains and desires are equal.

Whenever I get my teeth cleaned at the dentist, he pitches Invisalign because my top front tooth juts out a bit. Sure, perfect top teeth would be nice and I always tell him I'll think about it, but it's a lot of money to simply push one tooth into place. Then one morning I woke up with pain and swelling in the back of my mouth. An impacted wisdom tooth was infected, and it was killing me. I called the dentist right away to get it removed. It cost about as much as Invisalign, but I would have paid more if I had to. Because my pain was urgent.

Similarly, your buyers have pains they can tolerate like a crooked front tooth. And pains they can't ignore, like a throbbing, infected molar. You want to focus on their most urgent pains and desires that light a fire under your buyers' butts to get up and make a change. Otherwise, they'll keep tolerating the status quo.

For example, I consulted with a leading collaboration software that helped teams work together more effectively. Their buyer wanted to create a more inclusive culture where people felt they could contribute openly. But they had a more urgent pain to contend with first: overall productivity was down because everyone was stuck in back-to-back meetings.

People were reminded of it every day as they logged in to yet another meeting, and it was creating an undeniable problem for the wider business. The desire for a more inclusive culture paled in comparison.

Now, I'm an optimist who tends to gravitate toward the positive in almost every situation. Personally, I'd rather focus on desire than pain. But human psychology has proven that people are more motivated by solving or avoiding pain. You want to highlight the most urgent pains and desires. They'll serve as the foundation for your work in later chapters.

How to tell that your pain or desire is urgent:

- It's a common reason why prospects reach out to sales.
- It gets mentioned a lot in product reviews.
- It maps directly to a critical business goal or need.
- It reflects a deep personal aspiration or goal.

Make sure the pains and desires are something your product can actually solve. For example, one of the desires that came up for the collaboration software was "I wish we didn't have to have meetings anymore." A totally legit (and relatable!) desire, but not something the software could actually deliver. We'll get into this more in the next chapter.

## It Ain't Always about the Money

What's urgent to you might not be urgent to your buyer. Try not to make assumptions.

I worked with a pricing software company that helped golf courses use dynamic pricing to make more money from each tee time. Just plugging in their software was helping golf courses increase revenue by 6 to 9 percent—without adding any extra work! You'd assume that "increasing revenue" would be the ultimate goal of everyone, everywhere. But it wasn't. The buyers were busy golf course managers. And in customer interviews, we learned that these folks didn't care as much about revenue (after all, they didn't own the course)—they were more interested in getting away from their computers and having one less thing to do. To them, less work was far more motivating than a 6 percent increase in revenue.

It seemed totally counterintuitive to me, but I went with what mattered to the buyer. We anchored the messaging on this idea, and it performed really well.

Customer research is the best way of getting out of our own assumptions and understanding what your buyer truly wants and needs. In the next chapter, we'll explore how to connect them to your product's best features.

## A PUNCHY PEP TALK

Figuring out your buyer's urgent pains and desires takes time and depends on your access to customers. I don't expect you to go out and do every piece of messaging research all at once. Whatever you can do today to understand your buyer better than you did yesterday is great. Only have time to chat with one customer or speak to a salesperson for thirty minutes? Fantastic—it might reveal a valuable insight you were missing.

Messaging research is not all-or-nothing. Do a little bit, every now and then, to keep getting closer to your customer.

# Automox Gets Real with Technical Buyers

AUTOMOX IS THE leading IT automation platform for modern organizations. The platform helps organizations save time, reduce risk, and slash complexity by automating updates on all their endpoints (devices to you and me).

With a solution so sophisticated, it would have been easy to lean hard into the tech talk with this client. Their buyer is very technical and skeptical of big, showy claims and other marketing fluff.

But through our process, we discovered some deeply human needs and wants this buyer had—things that went way beyond the usual technical jargon. They wanted to stop spending all their time on a million little manual tasks. Instead, they wanted to work on big, strategic projects that let them play a larger role in their business. They had pains and desires, just like anyone else does.

So we played into that emotion. We touched on what it felt like when you were buried in tasks or were up all night worrying about vulnerabilities in the network. Automox was the only company in its category that was taking that approach—and it worked.

They started making more sales, winning customers' hearts and minds simultaneously with an authentic message. They could see that this approach was working, and that influenced the rest of their marketing efforts. They could run with it with confidence.

Automox used the messaging we created together for two years—practically a century in tech messaging years. Justin Talerico, Automox CMO, told me that this messaging worked so well because buyers felt invited in—Automox was sharing their solution, not selling it.

"Now we're getting five times the opportunities for the same marketing spend—and that's the power of speaking our ideal customer's language," Justin said.

# ADD THE SECRET SAUCE

**Connect your product's best qualities to your customer**

**N**OW THAT YOU understand your buyer's real pains and desires, it's time to connect them to the things your product can uniquely deliver. This is where punchy messaging lives—at the intersection of your buyer's motivation and your product's best qualities.

We're finally going to talk about the wonderfulness of your product! But we're not going to cover absolutely everything about it. Instead, we're going to focus on your product's best qualities: the unique features and aspects of your product that directly benefit your customers. We're looking for the very best things that will entice buyers to learn more. It's like how a movie trailer highlights the funniest or most action-packed scenes to entice people to go see it. In three short minutes, it gives you a complete sense of the movie—in fact, after watching a good trailer, I feel like I've seen the whole thing!

That's what we're going for when we message your product. We want to highlight its best qualities that will inspire your buyer to take the next step, whether that's reading more on your website, requesting a demo, or reaching out to sales. Remember, punchy messaging goes outside in, so we're going to choose the best qualities and see them through your customer's eyes: through benefits and value propositions.

## Sing Your Product's Praises

Start by identifying your product's best qualities—unique features and aspects that directly benefit your customers. This could be the product's secret sauce that differentiates it from other similar solutions, for example, super-fast processing times. Or it could be something your product does better than others, like a radically easy user interface in a sea of complex dashboards. Keep in mind that a best quality isn't an under-the-hood technical thing that doesn't directly connect to a benefit. (For example, I'm sure that highlighting a proprietary algorithm that runs behind the scenes has never gotten anyone to purchase hundreds of seats for a B2B SaaS platform.) And it's not an unsubstantiated claim like, "We have the best customer experience."

I once worked with a SaaS company that offered a digital workspace for lawyers and legal teams. Their customers were new to the workspace concept of having a digital hub for all their apps and docs. When I asked the team what was the thing that consistently made customers go "Wow!" they shook their heads: "Oh, it's just the main dashboard where they can see all their work in one place."

I could hear the disappointment in their voices. Their product team had all kinds of fancy AI-powered stuff in the software that they wanted to talk about. But the most basic thing the platform did—bring everything together on one screen—was what customers consistently raved about. The team desperately wanted to dismiss it in favor of highlighting more exciting, advanced, and new features. But I told them anything that gets a consistent "Wow!" out of people is part of what makes your product unique to your audience. If they all love it, it's a good indication that more people like them will love it, so we focused on this aspect of their product, and it attracted more customers. This initial "wow" factor was key in getting people to grasp what this new work-space thing could mean in the context of their lives.

Tech companies often see the world several years into the future. Comparatively, your customers are living in the past. They're often just coming to terms with the basics. This is another example of meeting your customer where they're at. You want to stay true to who you are, but you also want to talk about what has the most value to your customer.

## Brainstorm Benefits and Value with the "So What?" Game

Once you've figured out your product's best qualities, you want to look at them from your customer's point of view by translating them into benefits and value propositions. A fast and fun way to do this is by playing the "So What?" game.

Imagine sitting across the table from a bored teenager on their phone. Your goal is to get them to understand why your quality is so cool. (If you have your own bored teen at home, you probably know where this is going.) Every time you give them a good reason why your best quality is so great, imagine them shrugging and saying, "So what?" This means you have to dig a bit deeper to top the last thing you said. And they'll still say, "So what?" You keep going back and forth this way until you can't come up with any more reasons why your product's best quality is so great. (Spoiler alert: this typically happens somewhere around "increase revenue.")

Let's use the example of an AI chatbot for recruiters that appears on a company's career website. I'd start by explaining that "it lets you have real-time conversations powered by AI with candidates on the recruitment site." (So what?)

"So you can automate the manual part of screening candidates." (So what?)

"So you can speed up your screening process by asking candidates questions while they're on your career site." (So what?)

"So you can engage talent at the right time." (So what?)

"So you can hire the best candidates." (So what?)

"So you can exceed your KPIs for talent acquisition." (So what?)

"So you can help grow the business with the right people." (So what?)

The cool thing about this game is that you'll end up with a list of benefits and value propositions. Your brainstorm will likely be VBF in reverse—starting with the feature, moving into benefits, then expanding into value territory.

Write down all your "so whats." Then star the benefits— these are the superpowers that give your customer new things they can do, be, or feel, thanks to your product's best qualities.

Next, underline the value propositions—these are the big wins that multiple benefits help them achieve.

### PLAY THE "SO WHAT?" GAME WITH OTHERS

Like most things, playing the "So What?" game with colleagues will yield rich results. I've played this game with marketing teams for years, and it's amazing how different folks come up with different answers. You'll get more out of this exercise if you do it with others—even better if they don't know much about your product or feature. This will keep you honest and force you to dig deeper.

## Circle the Ones That Matter Most to Your Customer (and Meet Them at Their Level)

Once you have your list of benefits and value propositions, it's time to zero in on the strongest ones. It's easy to generate lots and lots of benefits and value propositions and then start drowning in the different things you could say—and feel like you have to say them all. But remember, punchy messaging isn't about saying it all, it's about talking to one person—your A+ customer—and showing them that you get them. You accomplish this by focusing on the benefits and value propositions that matter most to them. And making sure those benefits and value propositions resonate based on their tech-savviness and experience (which you learned about in Chapter 2). This means you want to think about the altitude of the benefit and value you've chosen.

**Find the intersection
of what your buyer
really wants and
what your product can
uniquely deliver**

"Altitude" is the word I use to measure how high-level and broad, or technical and specific, the message is. For example, a message that's too high in the sky is often lofty and vague. It focuses on a big, broad value that many other solutions could claim, like "increase revenue"—and is quite far from what your feature can actually deliver. At the other end of the spectrum, a message that's too low in the weeds is too close to the feature and functionality level. It focuses on what's in the solution and how it works, like "embed AI-curated data directly into your system"—which doesn't show a buyer why they should care.

When you play the "So What?" game, you create benefits and value propositions that go from low to high altitude. You want to choose the benefit and value proposition that's at the right altitude for your customer: not too high in the sky and not too low in the technical weeds. Like Goldilocks, you want to find that in-between to get it juuuuust right. As a rule, the more technical your buyer, the lower in altitude you want to go while still showing the value to them. And the more business-focused your buyer, the higher in altitude you want to go—without straying too far from what your product actually delivers.

Here's an example from a Punchy Training Workshop, where a marketer was running through the "So What?" game for one of her product's best qualities: AI fraud detection for credit card and loan applications. Her A+ customers were the heads of risk at major banks and credit card companies—they weren't particularly technical and were unaware of AI solutions for fraud detection because my student's company was the first in this nascent category.

In her "So What?" game, she came up with the following:

1  So you can have AI-powered, real-time fraud detection

2  So you can detect fraud faster

3  So you can save time detecting fraud

4  So you can detect fraud that can't be found in manual document reviews

5  So you can save the headaches of fraud and credit losses

6  So you can reduce risk

7  So you can increase company revenue

Number one (like in the beginning rounds of many of the "So What?" games) was too low in the technical weeds for their buyer, who might only have a vague sense of what "AI" means. On the other end of the spectrum, numbers six and seven were too high in the sky. Risk reduction and revenue increase were too many steps removed from what the feature actually delivered.

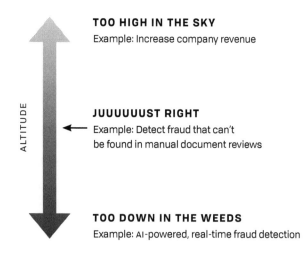

**TOO HIGH IN THE SKY**
Example: Increase company revenue

**JUUUUUUST RIGHT**
Example: Detect fraud that can't be found in manual document reviews

**TOO DOWN IN THE WEEDS**
Example: AI-powered, real-time fraud detection

ALTITUDE

In the middle (number four) was a benefit that was juuuuuust right: the ability to detect fraud that can't be found in manual document reviews. This connected to their buyer's urgent pains and met them at the right altitude: doing their work manually, without the aid of AI software.

It's all about finding that intersection between what your buyer really wants and what your product can uniquely deliver.

## How Do I Balance Where Our Product Is Today and Where It's Going Tomorrow?

What if some of your product's best qualities haven't launched yet? When can you talk about them in your messaging strategy?

This is a common conundrum for high-growth tech companies who are moving fast, just like when your A+ customer is evolving. You have a bigger vision of the roadmap, but the features aren't here yet, so how do you balance messaging what you have today versus where you're going tomorrow? It's about teeing up the future without overpromising.

What I've learned is that future features and releases don't just pop up out of nowhere. They're usually a natural evolution of the product and a piece of the overall vision. New features are often a faster, better way to deliver a benefit or value that's already being offered today. This means the essence of the new feature is already in the existing product. It's just being overlooked when you're focused on the functionalities that are currently live. But the golden thread that ties it all together? It's already there.

You can find it by asking yourself: What is the benefit of that new feature we're offering in the future? How are we delivering it today? And what are we doing today that has a similar spirit? For example, I worked with a SaaS company that helped people work together in a variety of ways, from brainstorming to performance reviews. In twelve months, the platform would have AI-powered prompts to help people perform tasks better. They would have live guidance, fully integrated into the platform experience. The idea was having proven resources and methodologies to improve how their customers did their work, which was unique for their space. So we asked what they were already doing that had a similar function.

Currently, they had a library of video resources that customers could use to learn how to do their work better. These videos offered the same benefit of helping users be more productive at work—the only difference was how that benefit was delivered via the product. So we included this benefit in their messaging to set the stage for the future product release.

We often get so focused on *how* we deliver a benefit (i.e., the feature) that we miss the fact that we are already delivering it today.

It's important to tee up future key product releases in your messaging. As long as you don't overpromise (or flat-out lie!) you're starting to raise awareness of what's possible, and what's coming, with your product. You're warming up people to the idea so when the product does launch, people are ready for it.

# A PUNCHY PEP TALK

In Punchy Training Workshops, the "So What?" game often takes marketers into new territory and explores ideas and angles they hadn't considered before. Through the exercise, many of them realize that they'd gotten into a rut with how they messaged their product. You might feel the same way. Try the "So What?" game, even if you feel like you have all the benefits of your best product features down. It's a creative exercise that may spark a fresh take.

# ThreatX Differentiates with Value

THREATX IS A leading API and app protection platform that helps enterprises block the most advanced cyber attacks.

While ThreatX offered a one-of-a-kind solution (no, really!), it was hard to communicate this over the noise of their crowded market. Every company was trying to explain how their technology was different, using the same buzzwords.

ThreatX offered two things that were unique in their market: their platform automatically blocked sophisticated attacks in real time, and they offered managed services at no extra cost.

When we interviewed customers, we found out that the value of these things went much deeper than ThreatX thought. Customers were relieved that they didn't have to constantly tinker and hand-hold the system, and they felt confident that their company was truly protected. Most importantly, customers got their nights and weekends back because they didn't have to manage the system themselves. These were the real reasons chief information security officers (CISOs) were referring ThreatX to other CISOs.

We used the customers as guides to help understand how they framed things. We built messaging around their phrasing—getting nights and weekends back and having ThreatX manage the solution for you. By focusing on the customer and value, we naturally simplified the company's messaging and avoided the typical buzzwords their competitors used.

The result was messaging that boosted their sales and marketing activities. Salespeople were able to simplify and connect with prospects by talking about the real, human benefits. And channel partners were able to easily tell the ThreatX story. In 2023, despite a very uncertain economic environment and a relatively flat year-on-year marketing budget, ThreatX saw marketing-sourced qualified pipeline opportunities grow in value by about 50 percent after deploying the new messaging. And their marketing-sourced opportunities grew in volume in 2023 over 2022.

# 5

## *STAKE YOUR CLAIM*

### Stand for one thing to cut through the noise

**T**HERE'S A shaved ice truck in our town that sends my kids into a frenzy whenever it rolls up to the local park. It's sugar-on-wheels—you buy a cup of snow-white ice, then self-serve as much flavored syrup as you want. The syrup stand is like a vision of heaven for any kid—they get free rein over fourteen nozzles flowing with sickly sweet, neon-colored nectar in flavors like lemon, dragon fruit, root beer, cola, and cherry. This rush of freedom, possibility, and sugar makes it impossible for my son to choose just one (or seven!) flavors.

How can an eleven-year-old be expected to choose between root beer and blue raspberry, anyway? There are just too many good choices—he doesn't want to miss out on something delicious. So he puts a little bit of everything in his cup. First root beer, then cherry. A glug of blue raspberry. Lemon and orange. Then a splash of dragon fruit, because that sounds cool too.

My son assumes that the awesomeness of each brightly colored flavor will bond with one another to create a mega-awesome taste combination. But instead, the colors slump down to the murky bottom of the cup. And he's the proud owner of a brown shaved ice that tastes the way it looks. After a few bites, the excitement is gone and he throws the thing away.

There's a brown shaved ice equivalent in messaging, too. It happens when you have too many different benefits and ideas swirled together until it all gets a bit murky and hard to swallow.

I remember coming across some brown shaved ice messaging on a cybersecurity platform homepage that included five different benefits in one long, thirty-five-word sentence. By the time I got to the end of the sentence, I'd completely forgotten the beginning of it, and I couldn't really tell you what the product did. There was just too much information to process at once. It's like the first day at a new job when you're trying to absorb all the new names, passcodes, and processes being thrown at you. By lunchtime, you've forgotten everything (and have a minor headache).

Brown shaved ice messaging confuses your buyer. When you try to stand for everything under the sun, people don't know what to think about you. And without a clear take-away, your messaging blends in with everyone else.

Why do so many companies do this? In my experience, it comes from a fear of missing something important in your messaging that a potential buyer might want to hear. (It's a close cousin to the fear of focusing only on your A+ customer.) So they talk about efficiency, risk reduction, *and* cost savings. All in one breath. Just to cover all the bases. Instead of letting fear drive your messaging development, have faith in what your product can uniquely deliver to your A+ customer—and give it the room it deserves.

## Your Unique Value Is Your Messaging Hook

Your product's unique value is the number one reason a buyer should choose your product over others. As with understanding your A+ customer, this step connects to positioning because it shapes how potential buyers think about your product. Clarifying your unique value will help focus your messaging and set you apart from other solutions. Buyers searching for a solution like yours want to get to the goods—they're looking for what makes you different. They can't digest 31 reasons why you're the best (this isn't a Baskin-Robbins), but they can remember the number one thing.

Your product's unique value is a main idea, *not* a customer-facing message. Think of it as the one thing you'd like your product to become known for, for example, the fastest performance or reliability. It will directly shape your product value proposition and benefits (which you'll tackle in the coming chapters). And this is not the time for subtlety—you must repeat this unique value over and over, metaphorically whacking people over the heads with it again and again for it to take hold in the market. That's how you break through the noise and get people to know what you are about.

Years ago, I worked with a popular online learning platform that offered hands-on training for engineers and developers. All their competitors talked about the same things: thousands of courses, expert instructors, exams and certifications, and a simple admin experience. There was a clear opportunity to stand out with something unique.

And my client *was* unique. Unlike other courses that focused on theory, my client's teaching style was hands-on and practical. Students got their hands dirty and applied techniques alongside instructors, which resulted in faster, deeper learning. And the lessons were enjoyable, because the company founders believed learning should be fun. Customers routinely raved about how engaging and effective the platform was.

My client's unique value was the concept of "learning by doing" which was more effective than other theory-led learning programs. Their unique value was core to their product vision; it was what their customers loved about their platform and what differentiated it from the competition.

We highlighted "learning by doing" in their product's new value proposition and drilled down into product benefits. As more and more buyers started looking for hands-on training providers, my client's platform stood out as the clear choice. Within months, the company was synonymous with "learning by doing" and had built the perception of being the top hands-on learning provider.

Their competitors eventually started copying their language and throwing "learning by doing" into the mix of their other messages. But the competition's copycat approach couldn't shift the market perception that my client's platform was the clear number one choice, or disrupt their year-over-year growth.

# Elevating the one thing that makes your product unique **is essential**

## Three Perspectives That Shine a Light on Your Product's Unique Value

Elevating the one thing that makes your product unique is essential to your messaging strategy. You can find it by looking at three perspectives: your company's, your customers', and your competitors'. I developed this brainstorming exercise to help you find it.

### Your Company's Perspective: What's at the Core of Your Product?

Your product's unique value is often directly connected to your company or product vision—that is, why you built it in the first place. It's about connecting to who you are as a company. Sounds obvious, but it's easy to lose sight of it through the demands of pursuing high growth. Quickly evolving markets, new competition, and innovation can distract you from your vision.

Think about the core problem you're solving and your way of solving it. What makes it unique compared to others? If you're in a new category, this could be a true differentiator that's not available elsewhere. And if you're in a more mature category, this could be a comparative differentiator, something you do that's similar to others, but superior.

For example, I worked with a cybersecurity company that had a remarkable approach to their technology around protecting APIs and applications. For years, they had been finding growth with a specific type of customer—a security person in a midsize company who knew they needed this kind of protection. They also knew this person didn't have the expertise or time to manage it themselves.

My client offered proactive software and service that took the task—and worry—off their plate completely. This was very different from other solutions that didn't offer this kind of support.

Meanwhile, a new category of startups popped up near them in an adjacent technology. The new startups had a different buyer and spoke more to developers—but they were getting a lot of funding and attention. My client couldn't help but feel the pressure to compete against these companies as well, and it was confusing their messaging.

I could see it happening—they were caught between two identities: the one that was true to who they were and a new one that they felt they should be. I asked them who they really were as a company, what was true to their technology, where they were going, and their growth goals.

I gave them permission to realize that their unique value was what they always set out to be: a great technology, with services included, so people could get advanced protection without worrying about it. They gave people their nights and weekends back. And they were good at it.

They felt great relief in knowing this was it. Sometimes we need permission, or a step back, to remember that we're doing exactly what we should be doing. You don't want to abandon who you fundamentally are (unless that is your agreed-upon business strategy). We doubled down on this unique value, which brought clarity to their messaging. And they grew their existing customer base even faster than before.

Returning to who you are as a company—and what makes your product great—is often where your unique value lies.

## Your Customers' Perspective:
## What Do They Routinely Rave About?

Anything your customers always say they love about your product is a good indicator of unique value.

For example, I worked with a company in a highly technical space in endpoint management (an industry term for handling the oodles of devices enterprises have to juggle). They were up against a lot of big software companies with classic tech messaging that was all about the robust features, the AI, and the innovation. But the truth of those solutions was that the power came at a cost of complexity. The IT team was wasting hours of their lives trying to manage all these endpoints. It was so complex; it was practically a full-time job to maintain the solution.

That's why people loved my client's offering. It was like hitting "the easy button" on this kind of solution. You could get up and running in minutes, you didn't need a manual to figure out how to use it, and it got the job done. The simplicity meant they didn't have to worry about it. And it was what every customer I spoke to on the phone talked about.

The company hadn't adopted this message before because part of them worried that being perceived as "easy to use" would make them look simplistic. But it was what every customer wanted. And so this idea of being the "the easy button solution" became the product's unique value. From value proposition to benefits, we showed how it was easier than other solutions—and they quadrupled their growth after two quarters.

Ask your customers why they chose your solution and what they think makes you different from others. Their answers will point you toward your product's unique value.

### Your Competitors: What *Aren't* They Talking About?

As your product's unique value begins to take shape, you'll want to see how it compares to the other voices in your market with something I refer to as "a competitive messaging audit." By putting your main competitors' messaging beside yours in a table, you'll get a sense of how other companies are talking about their product and whether your product's unique value is truly unique in your market.

Create a simple table with five columns and two rows. Choose your top five competitors (ideally the ones that most often come up in sales calls) and capture the following for each company:

- **Unique value:** What is the number one reason to choose the company or product? (This is typically found at the top of homepages or in the headline of a Google description.)

- **Main messages:** What are the most prominent benefits or outcomes mentioned? (These are the main bullets or messages typically found further down the webpage after the unique value.)

Once you have everyone's messages in one place, you can easily spot repetition and well-worn themes to avoid. For example, if you're a sales tech product, you might find that four out of five competitors have a main message of "close deals faster"—so this wouldn't be a strong choice for your product's unique value.

Also, take note of anything that's not being said. For example, if your product's unique value is related to how your platform gives IT teams confidence—and no one else

# Don't get too swept up in what competitors are saying

is talking about that—then it could be a potential candidate to highlight.

One word of caution: please don't get too swept up in what competitors are saying. Your product's unique value shouldn't be wholly defined by the language on a competitor's website. (I remember a past client thinking they couldn't use the word "growth" anywhere in their messaging because their direct competitor had it in a headline!)

Other companies don't have it all figured out, and they don't own particular words either. There's a chance that your value proposition language has appeared somewhere on other webpages—there are only so many words to go around. This is just an exercise to help you gauge possible routes and opportunities.

## Eventually You Have to Choose Just One Thing

Once you've looked at all three perspectives, your product's unique value might be glaringly obvious to you. Or, you might feel like you're drowning in too many ideas. If you're in the latter camp, keep refining your brainstorm. Look for common themes that repeat across at least two of the three perspectives. Throw your ideas on the wall. I mean that literally—I like to write ideas on sticky notes and slap them up on the wall. From this vantage point, you can easily spot if some themes are related, or if you're just saying the same thing in different ways.

Now for the really hard part—deciding which unique value to use. If you're like me and prefer to rip the bandage off as quickly as possible, ask yourself: "If we could be known for just one of these things, which one should it be?"

That forces you to decide which is the most powerful unique difference based on your product vision, what customers think, and what the rest of the market is saying.

If that feels like too much too soon, you can take it slower by removing them one by one. For example, if you have five themes, start by asking yourself which one you can safely take away. Remove it, reassess your four, then do it again. Keep doing it until you're down to one. I promise your product's unique value is in there, waiting to be seen. I've never worked with a company who didn't have one—but I've worked with plenty who struggled to agree on it and go all in. Because it's hard to stand for one thing when there's so much noise coming at you.

For example, I was running a messaging workshop with a company whose integration platform was incredibly robust. Technical buyers loved the platform's heavyweight solution because of the in-depth features that solved the needs of large, global enterprises. But their market was getting crowded with younger, "cooler" startups talking about their lightweight, no-code solution that any business user could master. My client felt the pressure to talk about those things too. I pointed out that you couldn't be both a heavyweight and a lightweight solution, just like a person can't be tall and short at the same time.

"Which one feels most true to your platform, and who you are as a company?" I asked.

Without hesitation, they agreed that they were the heavyweight solution. It was who they had always been, and why they were the darling of technical buyers. Through that lens, their unique value emerged around solving the complexity of enterprise integrations.

Remember, your product or feature was built to solve a special problem in a special way—and that's often where its unique value lies. Look within and listen to what your customers say to find it.

## A PUNCHY PEP TALK

Unique value means sacrificing lots of nice things you could say about your product to let one *great* thing shine. And no one likes sacrificing nice things, which is why most companies continue to message absolutely everything.

Let your faith in your customer and your product's unique value be stronger than the natural fear of missing out. Imagine how incredible it will be in the future when your product or company is synonymous with the unique value you've chosen.

Remember that choosing one idea doesn't mean you can never ever mention the other nice things about your product. Some of them might be expressed in benefits. Others may live in sales and marketing assets for people who are further into the buying cycle.

The role of messaging is to open that first door to your product and invite folks in to learn more. And your unique value sets the tone for your messaging framework, which we will dive into in the next chapter.

# Loom Doubles Down on Async Work

LOOM IS THE leading video messaging platform for creating and sharing screen recordings. During the pandemic, millions of people turned to Loom for a new way to communicate and connect with others in the new remote world.

Loom was ready for new messaging that supported its rapid growth in the enterprise and to differentiate it from other solutions. But with so many valuable use cases and benefits, it was challenging to focus on one unique difference (it's a good problem to have).

We looked at what was core to Loom's vision, things customers routinely raved about, and how competitors were talking in the market. And a golden thread emerged: Loom gave people a better way to work together asynchronously.

Customers loved that they could send a Loom instead of having a live meeting. Distributed teams marveled at how they could work across time zones in a faster, friendlier way. And companies were becoming more productive in the new distributed world. There was a clear opportunity to double down on how Loom made async work actually work.

In early 2021, "async work" was still a budding concept—which presented an opportunity for Loom to claim it. Their unique value proposition inspired memorable headlines like "meetings off, Loom on," which made it clear how it could help. And as the concept of async work grew more popular, so did Loom.

Since then, Loom has become synonymous with replacing meetings and is an essential tool for modern work, with upwards of twenty-five million users from more than four hundred thousand companies around the world who have recorded approximately 1.5 billion minutes.

# PART TWO

# WRITING

Write your messaging with new confidence.
In this section, you'll learn formulas to write value
propositions and benefits, plus simple tips for punchy
writing, so you can conquer the blank page for good.

# 6

## MAP YOUR MESSAGE

**Draft your messaging document
and outline your plan**

**OW THAT YOU** know what matters to your customer and your product's unique value, I bet you're itching to hit that keyboard and start writing your messaging. But there's one more step I'd like you to take before you do: draft an outline of your messaging. (I promise it's for your own good!)

One of the most challenging parts of messaging is figuring out what to say about your product that will resonate with buyers. If you haven't nailed that down before you start writing, you're liable to go off into brown shaved ice territory. Because trying to figure out *what* you're saying and *how* you're saying it at the same time can send you down the wrong path (a long, winding, wrong path).

It's like going grocery shopping without a list.

I don't know about you, but I hate food shopping for the week. I rarely make the time to plan out the week's meals for my family of five because I find that kind of thing incredibly boring. Listing out ingredients to buy feels like extra work, so I skip the planning and head straight to the store to get the shopping over with as fast as possible.

But this is dangerous in a US supermarket, especially when you're hungry. Without a clear plan of what to buy, I wander aimlessly through the aisles, tossing random stuff into my cart (like Oreos, broccoli, and that yummy, salted chocolate that's on sale) that don't add up to a meal. With no clear list of ingredients, I might end up buying 68 percent of what I need for any given dinner. And I'm especially vulnerable to the siren song of snacks and other empty calories. The whole shopping trip ends up taking twice as long and costing twice as much as it should.

And when I get home, I still don't have everything I need to make a damn meal.

This is what happens when you start to write your messaging framework before you know what to focus on in your value proposition and benefits. Without a plan, you'll end up writing aimlessly, tossing in more words and ideas than you need—including junk—and none of it will add up to a clear, cohesive message.

You can avoid all that when you draft the outline of your messaging framework first. Then, when it comes time to actually write the messaging, you can focus all your effort on clear, concise, and compelling writing (and not waste any brain energy wondering if you're talking about the right thing).

## The Punchiest Messaging Framework You'll Ever Meet: The VBF Rule

Over the years, I've seen a lot of company and product messaging documents from all sorts of tech companies—from Tech Giants to early-stage startups. Sure, they're all a bit different, but they share one big problem: there's waaaaaay too much stuff inside them. Field after field of value drivers, elevator pitches, benefits, capabilities, proof points, features, problem statements. The most important parts—the value proposition and benefits—end up being completely overlooked. It's the opposite of punchy.

The problem is all this extra *stuff* distracts from your efforts to build a clear and compelling perception in the market. Because a messaging document is meant to be shared with others—that is, colleagues, third-party agencies, and channel partners—when there are so many different things on the menu, everyone will order something different, leading to inconsistencies in your sales and marketing.

And on a personal level, it's stressful for marketers to be tasked with filling out a massive blank messaging document. I remember the first time I saw a company-approved product messaging template at a leading tech company that had thirty-two different sections to fill out. Even with all my years of experience, the thought of filling that sucker out kicked my anxiety into high gear and made me want to get on the next flight to Costa Rica.

Remember, the goal of punchy messaging is to show your customer how their life could be better (with the help of your product) in just a few sentences. You can do that with my super simple messaging document that follows the VBF rule.

The VBF rule boils down to this: one value proposition made possible by three benefits. Yup, that's it. This minimalist approach helps you simplify what matters most in your messaging, so colleagues and external partners can easily repeat it in the market again and again. Let's look at each component.

**Value proposition comes first.** Remember that a value proposition is a big win your customers can achieve with your solution. It's the number one reason why buyers should choose your product over alternatives and flows directly from the unique product value you uncovered in the previous chapter. A value proposition is often connected to a business-wide outcome or goal. In my *Star Wars* analogy from Chapter 1, a value proposition of the Force was to defeat the Empire and restore peace to the galaxy.

**Benefits come next.** They help show how your product delivers the value proposition. Remember how the Force enabled Luke Skywalker to control people's minds and fly ships with his eyes closed? Like superpowers, benefits are new things your customer can be, do, or feel with your product, and they map closely to your product's best features. Ideally, your benefits will be connected to the pains and desires of your A+ customers.

**Features come last.** Key features back up each benefit, showing how the product enables them. A bullet list of features beneath each benefit clarifies the connection between your product and customer benefits.

*Example: Sample VBF Messaging for*
*a Sales Engagement Platform*

| VALUE PROPOSITION: Simplify your path to predictable revenue | | |
|---|---|---|
| **BENEFIT 1** **Sell more, faster** | **BENEFIT 2** **Gain visibility into team performance** | **BENEFIT 3** **Create a playbook for success** |
| Cut time-sucking data entry and free your team to focus on what they're really good at: closing deals. | See your team's day-to-day performance, measure what's working, and sharpen your sales strategy. | Simplify daily workflows and put best practices on repeat, so everyone performs like your best rep. |
| FEATURES | FEATURES | FEATURES |
| · Email sequencing<br>· AI assistant<br>· Salesforce integration<br>· Task automation | · Real-time analytics<br>· Coaching insights<br>· Custom dashboard<br>· Reporting | · Workflow automation<br>· Reporting<br>· Task automation |

You might be thinking, *Pshht, no way is that enough to cover my company's complex platform and product portfolio.*

But I promise you it is. I've used this approach with billion-dollar public companies (that have sprawling product portfolios), early-stage startups, and everything in between. It works for messaging anything, from a minor new product release to a major platform launch. The framework of one value proposition delivered by three benefits is a scalable structure that can be applied to a capability, product, campaign, or use case—and you can even nest them to create a full messaging house of everything. (More on that later.)

And it all starts by clarifying the content of your value proposition and three benefits.

Here's how to think through the process.

## 1. Look for Connections between Your Customer's Urgent Pains and Your Product's Best Qualities

For messaging to resonate, it needs to highlight things your customer really, really wants that your product can uniquely deliver. You've already started brainstorming these individually in Chapters 3 and 4. We're going to take it a step further now by looking for connections between your customer's most urgent pains and desires and your product's best qualities.

Let's look at an example for a made-up sales engagement solution whose A+ customer is a sales director at a midsize company.

One of the sales director's most urgent pains is needing to get his entire sales team to hit their targets each quarter—almost everyone needs coaching to improve their performance. On a personal level, our sales director loves helping his team develop their skills and be more successful. He just wishes he had more time in his busy job to do it.

Now let's look at one of the product's best qualities: coaching intelligence that monitors the sales team's work and surfaces opportunities to improve performance. It serves up pointers that the sales director can use to have quick, fruitful coaching conversations, so he can give concrete feedback to help people do their job better.

There's a clear connection between what the sales director really wants—to be a good coach and help his team hit their targets—and what the product uniquely delivers—coaching insights to help salespeople improve their performance. This connection signals a potential key theme in your messaging.

Here are more examples of connections:

| Urgent Pains and Desires | | Product's Best Qualities |
|---|---|---|
| I need salespeople to stop wasting precious selling time on data entry. | → | Automates manual tasks so salespeople can focus on what matters. |
| I need all my reps to learn how to perform like my best reps. | → | Identifies the sales activities that work so you can roll out across your team. |
| I need to create a sales strategy based on data, not on what we think works. | → | Monitors and measures what's working in your sales campaigns. |

Go wide and brainstorm as many connections as you can—you'll refine them in the next step.

## 2. Distill Your Connections into Key Themes or Ideas

Next, you want to group similar and/or repeated connections into key themes. If you're messaging something big, like a platform, expect to have more themes than if you're messaging something smaller, like a new feature.

Here are examples of key themes based on connections for the sales engagement software:

A theme of "efficiency" emerges from connections around automating data entry, reducing manual tasks, saving reps time, and focusing on sales activities proven to work.

A theme of "visibility" emerges from connections around measuring the effectiveness of sales activities, getting a real-time view of how reps are performing, and spotting potential issues early.

Some of your themes might slightly overlap, like "better productivity" and "efficiency," but don't worry about that for now. The goal is to look for the main ideas emerging from your brainstorm.

## 3. Choose the Theme of Your Product's Value Proposition

First, decide what your product's value proposition is going to be about at a high level. Remember that a value proposition is the big win your customer wants to achieve. It's your ultimate promise to customers that sets the stage for your benefits. From the themes you identified among your connections, it should be easy to spot. That's because it will be the one that connects most clearly to the unique value you discovered in Chapter 5. It should also be echoed in some of your other key themes. Don't worry about wordsmithing at this stage—just aim for a rough idea. If you're torn between two ideas, put them both down for now.

For example, I might have two potential themes for the sales engagement platform's value proposition: "easier sales" and "predictable revenue growth."

# Get ruthless about what truly matters **to your customers**

## 4. Choose the Themes of Your Product's Benefits

After establishing your product's value proposition theme, you want to look at the themes again and find the three that drill down into benefits that make it all possible. These benefits directly underpin your value proposition and go a level deeper on how your product or company delivers that one big win (without diving into the mechanics of it all).

While your product likely offers many benefits, these are the ones that are most unique to you and critical to your customer. As a rule, the more unique a critical benefit, the more likely it will feature in your messaging.

Outline three themes that, together, provide a good overview of what's possible with your product. Here are examples of three benefit themes for our sales engagement platform:

1 More time for selling
2 Keep boosting performance
3 Scale what works

Finally, list the relevant features that deliver each benefit theme.

## Can I Have Four (or More) Benefits?

Choosing just three benefits is an exercise in sacrifice—which is why more than half of the leadership teams I've consulted with have asked me if they could break this rule and have four (even five!) benefits in their messaging.

Look, I don't want you to keep it to three because I'm an ogre—it's just that there's magic in the number three.

It's big enough to show the range of what's possible with your solution, but still small enough to be digested and remembered by your audience. People actually have a hard time recalling four or more things about your product or company. Landing on three benefits forces you to prioritize and get ruthless about what you can uniquely deliver that truly matters to your customers. It also provides guardrails for discussion if you're doing this with a group. It's the opposite of design by committee, where everyone throws something in and we try to say it all.

If you go for four benefits, I won't come after you with the messaging police. But I do have a cautionary tale for you: I once let my rule slide for a VP of marketing who had become a friend. It was our second time working together and he asked very nicely if they could have four "just this once." I relaxed and said, "Sure."

A year later, he came back to work on their enterprise messaging and he requested to keep it to three benefits. No, not requested, *insisted*. "We tried to do four, but it ended up being too much. We lacked focus and there was too much to juggle. I don't know why, but it just didn't work."

I nodded and tried to suppress a smug smile. Little did he know he was validating future-me to force thousands of other marketers to keep it to three (*mwah ha ha...*).

Don't just take my word for it. Challenge yourself to get it down to three benefits—you *can* do it.

## Move Themes Around Until They Tell a Cohesive Story

Despite being a creative person, I'm pretty hopeless at interior decorating. I buy random stuff that I like, but have no clue how to put it together. My friend is an interior designer, so I roped her into helping me decorate my home office after my shopping spree of random pictures and objects, like a forty-dollar glass cloche over a succulent. I couldn't for the life of me figure out how to arrange them in my room without making it look like the cops had just been riffling through my place with a search warrant. There was too much crap on one shelf and not enough on the other. The statue was too big on the table; the plant was too small in the corner. It looked like I'd bought all the wrong stuff, so I told my friend we could just return everything and start over.

She waved off my suggestion and started fiddling around the room at light speed, moving a plant from a shelf to the floor, tossing out a framed picture I didn't like anymore, finding a home for a random book in the corner of a shelf. Every few minutes, she'd pause, stand back, and look at everything for a quiet moment, then fiddle again. This went on for two hours until she stopped and surveyed my new perfectly styled space. Miraculously, all those different objects now made sense together. Turns out I hadn't bought all the wrong stuff—I just needed to put them in the right place.

When I asked her how she did it, she said, "I just kept moving things around until it finally made sense together as a whole."

I love this, because it's true of drafting your messaging outline, too. You have to fiddle around with the individual themes until they make sense together and tell a cohesive story. That means making sure your hierarchy is right and there are no missing pieces or superfluous ideas.

Here are some clarifying questions to help you with this necessary fiddling:

**Are you leading with the most important themes?** The more important a message is to your customer, the higher it should feature in your hierarchy. For example, you wouldn't want your third benefit to be more critical than your product's value proposition. Make sure you're leading with the most important win in your value proposition and put benefits in descending order of importance.

**Is the value proposition too vague for your buyer or market?** Sometimes your customer's big win ends up being too vague and many other companies could claim it, like "grow your business" or "save time and money." The more saturated your market, the more specific you'll want to be in your value proposition. We'll dive deeper into this idea in the following chapter when we (finally!) start writing the messaging.

**Do your three benefits give a good overview of what's possible with your product?** Or does it feel like something is missing? You want to cover the main points without sacrificing something that's key to your product or differentiated in the market. Sometimes, you just need to clarify a point within the benefit; other times, you may need to rework the whole theme itself.

**Are your benefits related but distinct from each other?** Or are they starting to blend together? For example, "productivity" and "performing daily tasks quicker" are too similar, and the latter is actually a subset of the former. If you have two benefit themes with the exact same set of features below them, it's a sign that they're too similar—and there's an opportunity to make them more distinct.

## How to Tackle Larger Messaging Frameworks with VBF

Despite its minimalist approach, you can use my punchy little framework to create larger frameworks for big platforms, product portfolios—and even a master messaging house for all your company's offerings. Simply apply the VBF structure at different levels and nest them accordingly. This lets you expand into more detail while keeping your focus tight.

For example, if you wanted to create a complete messaging house for your company, you'd start with VBF at the company level and define your one value proposition, three benefits, and bullet lists of relevant key features/products. Next, you'd apply VBF at the product level. Each product listed below the company benefits would get its own value proposition, three benefits, and bullet lists of relevant features. If you wanted to go even further, you could create a messaging framework for key features.

This nesting approach also works for messaging a large platform that includes individual products. You'd outline the VBF for the platform, then for each individual product.

Finally, there *is* some room for other components like Jobs to Be Done or customer proof points. It can be handy to have all that information in one place. Just be sure your product's value proposition and benefits remain front and center in your document, so your messaging stays clear and doesn't get lost in the mix of other supporting information.

# A PUNCHY PEP TALK

This step is the most strategic part of messaging, and it's a balancing act that may take some time. If you're creating messaging for a complex platform or a company with an expansive product portfolio, it can feel daunting to herd it all into one value proposition and three benefits. You might still think it's not possible.

But I know you can do this. Give yourself the freedom to fiddle around with this outline until it makes sense. And when you get to a place where themes fit together to tell a clear story, it brings clarity to the chaos of juggling too many things to say about your product.

# 7

## *MAKE IT STICK*

**Write a compelling value proposition and benefits**

**'VE BEEN** writing professionally for twenty-plus years, so you'd think writing this book was a breeze for me, right?

Ha! If only that were true. Writing this book was actually really hard. Distilling information and ideas into words isn't easy. There were times when everything I wrote sounded like crap and unclear, and the writing process felt never-ending. But I know I'm not the only one who feels this way about writing. Whenever I kick off Punchy Training Workshops, everyone shares what they're hoping to get out of the training, and almost every marketer in the group mentions these things.

Writing can feel challenging because it *is* challenging, no matter what your level of experience is. It's something every marketer is expected to be able to do, but most of us haven't learned how to do it since school. (And, let's face it, academic writing isn't even close to the same skill set we're supposed to have now, anyway.) Plus, the more you care about writing, the more likely you are to get stuck in your head and second-guess yourself during the process.

This is where outlines and writing formulas swoop in to save the day. In the last chapter, you did the strategic work of figuring out *what* to write about in your value proposition and benefits. Now, you're actually going to write them with the aid of my favorite formulas.

Formulas are like a springboard, allowing you to leap-frog over the heartache of getting started so you can land on a decent working draft faster. Approach these formulas like a young child would a new toy. Kids don't worry about playing "the right way" with it. They just pick it up, bang it around, and see what happens—with zero judgment of themselves. I want you to do the same with these formulas.

## How to Write Your Value Proposition

Your value proposition is a statement that clearly articulates the ultimate value customers can expect from your solution. Some folks mistake value propositions for brand taglines, like Nike's "Just Do It" or Zoom's "Meet Happy." While taglines convey a vibe, value propositions work much harder to communicate clear, tangible value to your customer.

It serves as the opening introduction for your product or company, so it must be strong enough to stand on its own. Realistically, it might well be the only thing your customer reads, whether in an ad or at the top of your website. Your value proposition needs these three attributes:

### Clarity

People should be able to read your value proposition once and understand it, no matter how technical your product is. Your value proposition should be clear and simple enough for a sixth grader to understand it. Avoid being vague or overly clever.

Yes: Block sophisticated attacks in real time.
No: Threat protection. Reimagined.

### Uniqueness

A value proposition reflects your unique value and shows people why they should choose you over alternatives. It highlights what makes your product special, which is critical when you're in a crowded market.

Yes: Attract leads with less effort.
No: Grow your business.

### Truth

No overpromising, truth-fudging, or wild claims. Your value proposition should be something your product can truly deliver. People's BS meters are at an all-time high, and over-the-top claims lead to a loss of trust in your company.

Yes: Increase your close rate by 21%.
No: Get 100% protection against cyber threats.

## Formulas for Writing Your Value Proposition

While they have similarities, each formula provides a slightly different angle for writing your product's value proposition. Try them all and see what you come up with. As you write, you may come up with a value proposition that takes you in a new direction or expands on what you had in your outline—that's perfectly OK. The writing process sharpens your thinking, so expect (and consider) new ideas.

### Formula 1: The Command One

This formula simply describes the big win that's possible for your customers (thanks to your product) in straightforward language—no frills necessary. Start with a verb, as if you're commanding your customers to achieve something great.

Fill in the blank in this prompt: *"Now you can _____ ."*
Examples:
*Now you can...*

* Build in-demand skills at your own pace. (online learning platform)
* Predict and prevent production losses. (industrial software)
* Get complex work under control. (work management software)

The command formula is a great all-rounder that works in almost any situation. It's a particularly good way to simplify headlines for highly technical products, and new and emerging technologies.

### Formula 2: The Aspirational One

This formula helps you tap into your customer's larger goals and personal aspirations to make your value proposition more compelling. As humans, we're all trying to become better versions of ourselves. We're not looking to buy software; we're looking for a positive change in our lives. This formula taps into your customer's emotions by illustrating how their life will change for the better.

Fill in the blank in this prompt: *"Imagine if you could _____ ."*

Examples:
*Imagine if you could . . .*

- Make every customer interaction count. (customer experience software)
- Accomplish more together, faster. (productivity software)
- Secure web apps with confidence, not complexity. (security software)

The aspirational formula is the best way to add emotion to your headlines and connect with your reader on a human level. It's also my go-to for writing value propositions for less-technical buyers.

**Formula 3: The Ultimate One**
This formula focuses on the ultimate end goal your customer is trying to achieve. You zoom out and show the big picture of a larger business goal.

Fill in the blank in this prompt: *"Ultimately, you will be able to _____ ."*

Examples:
*Ultimately, you will be able to . . .*

- Create a foundation for sustainable growth. (sales engagement software)
- Simplify cloud complexity. (observability platform)
- Build a culture of inclusivity. (employee engagement software)

The ultimate formula is great for B2B enterprise software, and value propositions that encompass multiple products.

## How to Write Your Benefits

Remember, a benefit is like a superpower: something new your customer will be able to do, be, or feel, thanks to your product. Benefits get more detailed about how you deliver the value proposition and help people quickly grasp why your product matters and what it could do for them. While there are many benefits to your product or solution, the benefits in your messaging focus on the most compelling ones that illustrate how your customer can do one of two things:

- Reduce or solve a meaningful pain
- Achieve a meaningful desire

A strong benefit has the following three characteristics:

**Empowerment:** Elevate your customer by leading with the cool new things *they* can do, not the cool new things your product can do. Avoid making your product look like the savior and champion your customer instead.

Example: Collaboration software

Yes: Get your distributed team on the same page with faster feedback, alignment, and decisions.

No: Our platform increases productivity by getting your distributed team on the same page.

**Directness:** Get straight to the point and show people what they can do. Avoid setting the stage with an introduction—just tell people what they'll be able to do, be, or feel.

Example: Contract management software

Yes: Decrease paper, printing, and handling costs by moving away from hard-copy reviews.

No: Digitizing processes can help you reduce costs. When you minimize hard-copy reviews, it enables you to decrease paper, printing, and handling costs.

**Concreteness:** State benefits concretely so you can picture them in your mind. This helps people understand exactly what you're talking about and apply it to their life. Avoid vague, abstract language—for example, intelligent workflow automation—and describe what benefits looks like in their lived experience.

Example: Patch management software

Yes: Remediate thousands of critical vulnerabilities in days, not months.

No: Transform endpoint protection.

## Formulas to Write Your Benefits

Your benefit should have a headline plus a supporting message that's one to three sentences long. I recommend using the command formula for the headline. Here are three different formulas you can use to approach your supporting message.

# A benefit is something new your customer can do, be, or feel

**The Big Picture**

This formula sets up the benefit as the key to unlocking a larger goal. This is a great way to tie your product to a meaningful business goal or personal aspiration. That's why this formula is great for audiences who aren't very technical and/or are unfamiliar with solutions like yours.

Fill in the blanks in this prompt: *"[Describe benefit], so you can [larger goal or outcome]."*

Example: Customer service chatbot

Resolve issues quickly and accurately the first time, so your customers become even bigger fans of your brand.

**Before and After**

This formula shows how your customer's situation will change for the better. The "before" part illustrates the current pain they're experiencing, and the "after" part shows how it could be solved. This formula is a great way to help people grasp the benefits of a new or emerging technology. Prompt: Brainstorm what your customer's life or situation was like before and after your product. Then put them next to each other in your message.

Fill in the blanks in this prompt: *"Stop [before] and start [after]."*

Example: Work management app

Stop bouncing from system to system and feeling bonkers along the way. In your workspace, your team can see everything at once—and handle it with ease.

### Benefit Progression

This formula breaks down a large benefit into three smaller ones—this is good for tackling company-level benefits. Break down your benefit into three consecutive super-powers. Remember, three is the magic number that shows breadth without overwhelming the reader.

Fill in the blanks in this prompt: *"You can [superpower 1], [superpower 2], and [superpower 3]."*

Example: Data security platform

Locate every threat, figure out what the attackers are after, and keep your data and systems safe for good.

## How to Choose the Best Value Proposition and Benefits

Once you've written a few options, how do you know which ones are the strongest? Use my rubric to figure out which ones they are—and which need more work. It will help keep you out of subjective criticism (e.g., "I don't like that one") and point you in the direction of the benefits and value propositions that are objectively stronger.

Rate each of the three value propositions and benefits from 1 (meh) to 5 (excellent) using the following criteria:

### Value Propositions

- **Clarity:** Can you read it once and understand it? Could a sixth grader understand it?

- **Uniqueness:** Does it connect to your unique value and stand out? (Check your competitive messaging audit.)

- **Truth:** Can we back up this statement with numbers or customer proof?

**Benefits**

- **Empowerment:** Does my benefit elevate my customer and show what cool new things they can do?

- **Directness:** Does it get to the main point without dilly-dallying or going off on a tangent?

- **Concreteness:** Does it have concrete detail, so you can picture it in your mind?

The higher the score, the better. Any value proposition or benefit that scores 10 or more is on the right track.

## Calibrate Your Messaging to Your A+ Customer

When I speak at conferences about leading with benefits and value, I often get asked if this is the right approach for sophisticated tech buyers who "hate marketing fluff," like developers.

I'd argue that most B2B buyers hate marketing fluff (we'll get into this in the next chapter). But tech-savvy buyers aren't too smart for benefits—they simply need more advanced benefits than a business buyer, like a CEO, would.

Your benefits and value proposition have to balance being understandable with being credible for your customer. And this will vary depending on how knowledgeable your customer is.

In Chapter 2, you established your A+ customer's understanding of a product or solution. This helps you understand exactly where your customer is at so your messaging can meet them in the right place. To do this, follow this basic rule: *The less they know about solutions like yours, the broader the message. The more they know about solutions like yours, the more specific the message.*

Let's take the example of CRM, a mature software category and common system in most businesses. If you were marketing the CRM to very small businesses, like yoga studios and dental offices, the buyer might be an administrative assistant or owner, and they might not know too much about CRMs. They may have heard of popular ones, like Salesforce, and know that they should have one. But this might be their first CRM. They're likely looking at a CRM to replace manual methods of tracking customers, like spreadsheets.

Because this buyer doesn't know a ton about CRMs, the messaging should be broader about the value of using one, like the ability to keep all your client communication in one place. These broader messages help your buyer understand why a CRM matters and what it could do for them. If you dove into a more advanced benefit, like workflow automation, it would be too much too soon.

On the flip side, if you were marketing the CRM to a buyer in a midsize tech company, such as a VP of sales who is well versed in CRMs, your messaging would need to be more specific. They've used CRMs before and already know all the high-level reasons to use one, so there's no point wasting time on messaging that covers the basics. (If you messaged "keep your client communication in one place" they would be like, "No duh.") Instead, you want to get more specific about how your CRM is different from others. For example, you might write benefits that touch on how your software alerts you to opportunities or speeds up workflows with AI.

Broader Messaging:

- Best for people who are less aware or experienced with solutions like yours
- Highlights why your solution matters, by focusing on high-level outcomes
- Typically encapsulates more than one feature

Example (project management for legal teams):

Always know where every project stands. Make legal a strategic part of the business, and stay way ahead of any issues.

Specific Messaging:

- Best for people who know a lot about solutions like yours
- Highlights differentiation by focusing on more specific benefits and value
- Often maps to a specific feature that's unique in the market

Example (API gateway for developers):

Maintain a reliable, secure infrastructure to avoid disruptions and outages that slow you down.

# A PUNCHY PEP TALK

Ernest Hemingway said, "The first draft of anything is sh*t"—and I hope you find his words as liberating as I do. Because not only does it mean you're totally allowed to write a terrible first draft of your messaging (hey, if it's good enough for Hemingway...), but it also proves a garbage first draft is a natural part of the writing process that you can—and should!—embrace.

My kids and I love hunting for agate in the sand of Oregon's beaches. At first glance, the pebbly sand looks gray and unremarkable. But when you take a sloppy scoop of it and put it through a sifter, big chunks of clear, beautiful agate appear. The gems were in the sand all along.

Your best ideas are like bright agate hiding in the gloopy gray sand of other thoughts. You have to toss a big clump of 'em on the page in order to sift through and find them. Get your ideas on the page without judging them or trying to make them word-perfect. Give yourself permission to write a long, crappy value prop and benefits. We'll continue to refine them in the next chapters.

# DITCH THE JARGON

## Edit your messaging for buzzwords and fluff

**W**HO AMONG US hasn't been guilty of trying to sneak a "carrot-based workflow" into our messaging at some point?

I was running a messaging workshop with the leadership team of a software company that sold to developers. While we discussed the unique aspects of their platform that helped developers be more productive (which was at the heart of what made them different from other solutions), the CMO kept talking about "carrot-based workflows."

The phrase stood out to me because I'd never heard it before, and it sounded... odd. It was my first vegetable reference in a product messaging workshop. I wondered if maybe I misheard him, but then he mentioned it again, as a key driver of productivity.

Should I have known what this thing was? I was a messaging consultant for tech companies, after all. Was I missing something here? I glanced at the faces of the other people in the Zoom call to see if they were confused too, but they were nodding along like people who knew what a carrot-based workflow was. I surreptitiously googled it in another browser, which only brought up cooking recipes using carrots. So I was left with no choice but to speak up.

"This may be a dumb question, but what is a carrot-based workflow?" I asked, feeling a bit naked. I braced myself for an obvious answer. The CMO smiled and explained that it was a term his team had made up to describe the specialness of the feature. "I've been using it for a while and I really like it," he added. A private DM from a colleague popped up on my screen: *Thank god you asked. I didn't know what he was talking about either!!*

His jargon was supposed to articulate the unique value around developer productivity. But instead, it confused everyone in the room, and made a few of us feel a bit dumb for a minute. And these two things are happening on a global scale in tech, all thanks to jargon.

## Jargon: The Sworn Enemy of a Clear Message

Jargon is the number one obstacle between technology and messaging that resonates with actual humans. This language tries to sound impressive, but doesn't really say anything at all. For example: "Leveraging best-in-class technology to transform business outcomes."

It sounds like one business robot talking to other business robots—rather than a person talking to other people.

Jargon is a lot like refined sugar. At first, it feels like a sweet way to communicate the power and innovation of your product—and you can quickly get addicted to the stuff. But they're empty calories that bloat your message with meaningless words. Just like refined sugar is secretly added to a lot of food, jargon lurks in most messaging documents, too. And it has serious negative effects.

Jargon hides the real value of your product. It tricks you into thinking you've conveyed some big, exciting value, when you haven't said much of anything. There's no clear meaning so people are left to hunt for the value on their own (if they can be bothered). It's confusing, boring, and a real waste of those precious few moments you have to get a reader's attention.

Jargon also creates skepticism and mistrust. Do you believe big, hyped statements about a revolutionary product? Neither do your buyers. One of my clients, a leader in the collaborative space, surveyed two thousand prospects in the enterprise to help inform their product strategy and messaging. One of the key recommendations out of the study was to get rid of jargon, which caused confusion and/or dislike in 49 percent of audiences. (I'm just surprised that number wasn't higher!)

Jargon is pervasive in tech, which means everyone is the "best-of-breed" solution or the most "seamless." Instead of highlighting what makes your solution so powerful and unique, jargon makes you sound like everyone else and blend into a crowded market.

That's why you have to ditch the jargon to make it punchy.

## How to De-Jargon Your Messaging

Jargon has a way of popping up in your messaging like weeds, no matter how good your intentions are. When we share our writing in Punchy Training Workshops, some marketers feel a bit embarrassed when they realize how much jargon crept in. And I always tell them there's no shame in it—we all use jargon because it's really hard not to.

It's an unconscious force. You can be focusing on your customer and trying to write a value-based message and then *BAM!* "Accelerate operational efficiencies" is staring back at you from the screen. As if it wrote itself.

You must be vigilant and look out for it. Here's how you can attack it one step at a time.

### Step 1: Hunt for Jargon in Your Messaging

Review your messaging and look for jargon, from the glaringly obvious "synergy" to the questionable "streamline."

In B2B tech, we've been using jargon for so long that we've developed different flavors of the stuff—four flavors by my count.

#### 1. Corporate-Speak

Examples: leverage, synergy, bandwidth, agility

This type of jargon is thrown around so casually in the B2B world that it's easy to overlook. (Let's face it, you've probably said "bandwidth" five times already this week.) I think we started using these to sound "professional" and "serious" in business. But fancy corporate-y words make you sound like a robot and definitely don't add any clarity—or spice—to your messaging.

#### 2. Buzzwords and Hype

Examples: transform, revolutionize, supercharge, game-changing, reimagine

Many tech brands lean on these words to communicate the power and innovation of their products, so it's no surprise they pop up the most in B2B messaging. They're meant to sound impressive, but they've lost almost all meaning. They're way too focused on glorifying your technology and ignoring your customer. And that's boring.

### 3. Internal Lingo

Examples: end-to-end ecosystem, composable automation, carrot-based workflows

As you might have guessed, this flavor of jargon is filled with the words and phrases teams make up themselves (often to describe something new). These words get bounced around in the internal echo chamber until they start to seem like they'll resonate with the market, too. But they just don't. Unfortunately, your customers aren't in your head or in your team meetings. They're mystified— so you have to spend more precious time explaining what your made-up word is trying to say.

### 4. Deep Tech Talk

Examples: augmented analytics, downstream systems, ML-defined data abstraction

This type of jargon is advanced, technical language that only an expert or day-to-day practitioner would understand. Remember, most B2B messaging addresses a buying group of six to ten people, so it's unlikely more than one or two of them will be enticed by technical language. The group probably includes more business buyers and decision-makers—who are focused on results and value. So deep tech talk will only serve to confuse (and bore) this crowd.

### Step 2: Translate What Your Message (Actually) Means to Your Buyer

Trade out jargon for more simple, human language that speaks to the real benefits of your solution. Use everyday words to tell the reader that you know what they're going through. Help them picture it in their mind so they can get a sense of relief.

For example, say you spotted the jargon "achieve operational excellence" in your messaging. What does this actually mean to your buyer? What does "achieving operational excellence" look like through their eyes? To them, it could simply mean their business is able to deliver consistent service.

So you'd rewrite "achieve operational excellence" to "deliver consistent service." This jargon-free phrase uses everyday words and focuses on the outcome. And that's much clearer and more compelling to your buyer.

Here's an example of how the messaging gains clarity without the technical clutter of jargon.

Before: Unleash the power of 5G with best-of-breed, multigenerational network infrastructure.

After: Move fast with 5G while preserving the value of your 3G and 4G networks.

## But What If My A+ Customer Uses Jargon, Too?

Whenever I preach about using less jargon, there's always someone who raises their hand and says they have to use jargon because they're writing for the enterprise, or developers, or IT.

# Jargon hides the real value of your product

And there is a nugget of truth to that.

I don't want you to go out of your way to avoid using an industry term familiar to your readers just because it sounds like jargon to your neighbor or your mom. Imagine talking about a threat protection solution without using the words "ransomware" or "zero-day." Or describing a recruiting solution without ever saying "talent acquisition." Or saying "application programming interfaces" instead of APIs. You often need a sprinkle of these terms to help frame up your solution for the reader.

You want to speak your customers' language to build credibility with them. But if you really think about it, is your reader using all deep tech talk all the time? Probably not. So use industry terms as needed to be accurate and understood, but always remember you're trying to connect with a human. They want to hear that you understand their problem and have a solution.

I wish I could offer you an exhaustive naughty list of jargon, but sadly it doesn't exist. "Workflow" might be jargon to an HR director but natural language to a sales ops director. If you're not sure, here's a quick "Is It Jargon? Test":

* Will it be universally understood by your audience?
* Is it meaningful to your audience?

For example, the word "omnichannel" might sound like a buzzword in isolation. But if I used it in product messaging for a martech solution aimed at B2B marketers, it would be both universally understood and meaningful to them. So I would consider including it.

If my messaging talked about "accelerating business outcomes," those same B2B marketers might understand the idea, but it wouldn't have a clear meaning. Some might think I was talking about increasing revenue; others might think about efficiencies. That would be a sign to find a clearer way to show the customer benefit.

## ⊹ PUNCHY TIP ⊹

### KEEP A JARGON BLACKLIST

When I work with a company that's struggling to break up with jargon, I give them a blacklist of words to avoid using. There are always a few common offenders! This makes it easier for people to identify them without having to figure it out for themselves. Eventually, these words won't even try to creep back into their writing—they'll know they aren't welcome there.

## Coined Terms, Category Names, and Other Famous Jargon

In 2005, HubSpot's co-founder Brian Halligan famously coined the phrase "inbound marketing" to describe their software's unique approach and point of view. The company became the leader of a movement that changed the marketing landscape forever—and made HubSpot synonymous with it.

Since then, many tech companies have tried to do the same with their own made-up name, hoping it catches on like wildfire in the market. This spawned a whole new wave of jargon, as companies attempted to coin a name for their new category, POV, or technological innovation.

But with so many competing solutions in the market, it's impossible for everyone to create their own category or movement that catches on. Behind every enviable success story are countless unmentioned failures. More and more, I meet with teams who had to abandon a coined name because it never took off—or worse—it confused the heck out of their customers. Like jargon, these names end up being meaningless and get in the way of understanding.

Coining a name is a gamble, and you have to put it out there again and again to see if it sticks. You have to give it time, budget, and solid marketing. If your company has a strong or contrarian point of view, then it might make sense to coin it and get it out there.

However, I recommend most of my clients consider clarity over coining. After all, that's the goal of messaging: to help people quickly grasp your product's unique value. Most of the time, simple, straightforward language will serve you better in accomplishing that goal than a made-up name.

For example, I worked with a cybersecurity company that had coined a name for their technical differentiation called "attacker-centric behavioral analytics." But it wasn't landing, because it was too jargony. It was hard to understand and impossible to remember.

Then during customer interviews, I heard customers describing the unique approach their own way. They called it "risk-based blocking," which described the outcome of the technical differentiation, rather than the technology itself. The words may not have been as impressive, but when people heard it, they intuitively got what it meant. Compare that to making someone decode your meaning.

And that's true in the majority of cases. However, if a coined name helps to drive your story, then go for it. If it confuses people, you're better off going for the human version.

## How to Convince Colleagues and Leadership to Banish Jargon

When I get on my soapbox about jargon at conferences, almost everyone in the crowd nods along eagerly. Then someone raises their hand and says, "I totally agree with using less jargon, but everyone in my company loves it. How do you convince them to let the jargon go?"

For many companies, jargon is so deeply ingrained in the workplace culture that trying to fight it feels like a losing battle. You fight hard to strip out the jargon in your one-sheeter, only to have a colleague write it back in. You try a more interesting approach on a landing page but get asked to add jargon to make it sound "more enterprise."

But after helping people from hundreds of companies use less jargon, I know there's a business case for doing it. Here are some talking points to pass on.

**You'll see real improvement in marketing campaigns:** I worked with one particularly jargon-plagued team in a Punchy training. This group took what they learned and applied it right away to paid campaigns. They saw a huge lift across the board because it was human and personal—not the same robotic language their prospects were used to reading.

**You'll be perceived as a modern company with a fresh take:** A website full of jargon is a legacy approach to messaging—it's just not cool anymore. These days, buyers want to connect with authentic companies and real people. Many software companies, like Asana, Slack, Dropbox, and Stripe, have proven you don't have to sound like a droid to be successful.

**You'll make your value accessible and clear to more people:** You know the phrase "A confused mind doesn't buy"? Well, that's true. A confused mind says, "Yikes. I can't deal with all that," and moves on.

**You'll stand out from other companies:** Using jargon makes you sound like everyone else. Focusing on clear, human messaging will make you stand out, especially in more technical arenas like cybersecurity, IT, and enterprise solutions. For example, after I helped a cybersecurity firm reduce jargon on their homepage, they increased demo sign-ups.

In my experience, you have to make a commitment to doing this as an organization.

One CMO we worked with hired us to teach his team of three hundred product marketers how to write simple, jargon-free messaging. We were (pleasantly) surprised by how big a priority cutting jargon was for a global org. They saw fantastic results—everyone on the team learned to write more clearly about their products, quicker.

Here's the beauty of their no-more-jargon decree:

- Now there's no argument as to whether people can use that technical jargon.

- Now everyone knows why simple, jargon-free messaging matters.
- Now there are fewer back-and-forth revisions with colleagues.
- Now the messaging is just plain better.

This all could happen because it came from the top. Going cold turkey on jargon as a group is the path to fewer rewrites—and a better connection with your buyers.

## A PUNCHY PEP TALK

When I speak at conferences about jargon, marketers always come up to me afterward and say they didn't realize how much jargon they'd been using until then. You might be thinking the same thing. It may seem like you suddenly need to do a lot of work to get rid of it all.

However, you don't have to banish every piece of jargon right this minute (that would be impossible anyway). Just do it little by little. The more you know about jargon, the easier it gets to spot. And once you start replacing jargon with clear language, it'll become second nature. After a while, you won't even have to think about it when you're writing messaging.

# PUNCH IT UP

**Make your messaging
clear and concise**

**W**HEN I WAS eleven years old, my teacher ran a weekly contest to help us remember our latest round of vocabulary words, like "contemplate" and "veracity." Whoever could fit the most new vocabulary words into one sentence won the illustrious Golden Paperclip Award—a giant yellow paperclip that dangled around your neck on a piece of yarn for the week.

Finalists in this prestigious award included sentences like these:

*"After four consecutive days of persistent rain, Jenny was reluctant to commence playing outside."*

*"Billy had adequate time to contemplate his unique circumstance."*

*"Dad's recurring grimace transmitted his stern viewpoint with veracity."*

Looking back, I suppose these sentences proved our loose understanding of each word's meaning. But we were more concerned with using big, fancy words than trying to communicate a clear idea because the most flowery, highfalutin sentence always won. Not to brag, but I won this contest so many times that my teacher gave me a plastic paperclip to keep so other kids had a chance of winning. Little did I know that this game would set me and my classmates on the path of long-winded, overly formal writing for many, many years. How you learned to write in school—big words and long sentences—shapes how you write in business. And if you were born before the internet (like me), then long-winded writing has been hardwired into your brain.

Practically every marketer I've ever spoken to about messaging has confessed this to me like it's a dirty secret: "My writing is too long because I struggle to be concise." And I always reassure them that concise writing doesn't just happen for the chosen few—it's the result of the editing process. Long-windedness is the starting point for all of us.

Expect your first value proposition and benefits draft to be too long. This chapter will give you simple techniques to trim down your messaging, so you can connect to your buyer in as few words as possible. And make it punchy.

## The Single Most Important Takeaway (SMIT)

Remember when I asked you to establish the main concept for your value proposition and benefits before you wrote your messaging? This helped frame your thinking and focus your writing. But once you started writing, I bet your concept got stretched out and layered with other ideas, didn't it? Because the more you know about the subject of your messaging, the more you tend to write about it. (The Curse of Knowledge strikes again!)

You can rein it all in by clarifying your Single Most Important Takeaway (SMIT) in every message. Your SMIT is the main point you want your reader to walk away with.

SMIT is all about focusing on the core idea in your message and removing all the other stuff that distracts from it. It helps your reader digest your message without drowning them in too many ideas.

Reread your messaging and ask yourself, "If my reader only remembered one thing, what would it be?" The hard truth is that you're lucky if your reader remembers even one thing, because their mind is ruthlessly filtering out excess information. And the more you put in front of them, the less they'll remember. This question helps you sacrifice the non-essential stuff so your most important idea can shine.

Here's an example of a benefit message for a made-up enterprise communication platform.

*Now you can reduce back-to-back meetings by working async across time zones and cross-functional teams. Increase productivity across the business by giving people the time and flexibility to do their best work without interruption. You can also easily capture and share knowledge across teams, for more effective onboarding and training.*

You'll see a bunch of ideas and outcomes in this effort. (No judgment, though.) As the marketer, I think all of the information is relevant and important. But if my reader will only remember one thing, what would I like it to be? The Single Most Important Takeaway would be the idea of "less meetings for more productivity"—because this connects to what my buyer wants the most and what my product can uniquely deliver.

Once you identify the SMIT, take out all the details and information that distract from it, and only keep (or add) detail that supports it. In this case, I'd remove the last sentence about capturing and sharing knowledge for onboarding and training. (These ideas are just crowding my SMIT and trying to steal the spotlight—they gotta go!)

*Now you can reduce back-to-back meetings by working async across time zones and cross-functional teams. Increase productivity across the business by giving people the time and flexibility to do their best work without interruption.* ~~You can also easily capture and share knowledge across teams, for more effective onboarding and training.~~

I know it's tough to delete good things about your product. But remember that this message isn't your one shot to say it all. Your deleted ideas may well live on in other marketing assets. Trust me when I say that the more you SMIT, the easier it gets.

---

### ⟡ PUNCHY TIP ⟡

#### JUST SMIT IT!

Long-windedness happens everywhere, not just in messaging. I encourage you to SMIT anything with words: a paragraph in a blog post, a slide in a presentation, a landing page, an email to your colleague. The use cases are endless! SMIT is a simple reminder to focus on what's most important for your reader.

## Short Is Bold

Once your SMIT is clear, you're ready to edit your messaging for conciseness. The more concise your message is, the bolder it sounds.

Practically every head of marketing I've ever worked with has told me they want their messaging to sound bolder. They want it to exude the confidence of a clear market leader. They want it to be clear that they're good at what they do, and they know what they're talking about.

Long-winded sentences have the opposite effect: they make you sound shy and unsure. A mouthful like "leverage over a dozen data destinations simultaneously" lacks the decisiveness of something more concise, like "use 12+ destinations at once."

So how short should your value proposition and benefits aim to be? Despite what you may have heard, there is no minimum word count rule for messaging. Aim to use as few words as needed to make your message understood. Here are my go-to ways to do it.

### Start Sentences with Active Verbs

Start your sentences with an active verb. It makes your reader feel like you're speaking *to* them, rather than *about* them, and champions the cool new things they can do, be, or feel with your product. When you start with a verb, you get to the point faster. It's common to set the scene with problem statements or preambles like "our platform is purpose-built to..." But this just pushes your point to the end of the message (and people might not make it that far). In messaging, most sentences should start with the active verb that illustrates the SMIT for your reader.

# Edit words like you would edit a wedding guest list

Before: The platform is designed to enable customers to run analytics on data that is stored in MySQL databases.

After: Run analytics on data that is stored in MySQL databases.

### Shorten Sentences

Studies from the American Press Institute nicely demonstrate the effect of sentence length on a reader's understanding of a story. When people read a story with an average sentence length of eight words, 100 percent of them understand it. When they read a story with an average sentence length of fourteen words, 90 percent of readers understand it. But when the average sentence length jumps up to forty-three words, less than 10 percent of people understand the story.

I've seen many B2B tech websites plastered with sentences in the thirty-to-forty-word range, which means no one's really understanding it. You can avoid this by deleting words that don't pull their weight in your sentences. Edit words like you would edit a wedding guest list. Imagine each word costs you eighty dollars. Just like you'd reconsider inviting your annoying second cousin and weird uncle, look at each word and ask yourself—honestly—if it needs to be there. Does your sentence lose meaning without it? Does it make the sentence better? If the answer is no, delete it—because inessential words add up fast.

Before: HR teams can easily create visually appealing career sites that better resonate with job seekers and meet their organizations' brand standards without having to purchase additional products or seek help from IT.

After: Create visually appealing career sites that meet your brand standards without needing help from IT.

Short sentences are clearly easier to digest than long ones. So keep your sentences under twenty words to make sure your message is understood.

### Swap Big Words with Little Words

Trade big, fancy words for short, simple ones. Instead of "utilize" try "use." Swap "implement" with "do." Not because your reader isn't smart enough to understand big words—but because they slow your reader down (sort of like wading through mud). Use big words intentionally, and only when a shorter one won't do. Otherwise, hit up your thesaurus for a simpler alternative.

Before: The platform is purpose-built to accelerate the identification, diagnosis, and resolution of issues across complex IT environments.

After: See, find, and fix issues quickly across your IT landscape.

*Punchy Swaps for Common Tech Words*

| Instead of... | Try This... | Instead of... | Try This... |
|---|---|---|---|
| Accelerate | Speed up | Visualize | See |
| Leverage | Use | Mitigate | Reduce |
| Identify | Find | Facilitate | Improve, ease |
| Utilize | Use | Ensure | Make sure |
| Implement | Do | Alternatively | Or |
| Enable | Let, allow, help | Optimize | Boost, improve, up |
| Provide | Give | Eliminate | End |

## Make It Spicy

Once you've shrunk down your message to the SMIT, it might feel like you've stripped off its personality. But this is your chance to spice things up a bit. Look for opportunities to add zing, interest, and personality to your messaging.

This is where messaging rubs elbows with copywriting—because you've got to differentiate from all the vanilla messaging out there. While purists might argue that messaging should be ultra-plain and nothing like engaging copy, I don't think this is helpful (or realistic) for many tech companies.

I created my messaging approach to serve the unique needs of fast-moving startups. My largest early clients (both of which are now well-known market leaders in sales tech) wanted clear messaging to differentiate and cement their positioning. But they also wanted messaging that people could put directly into marketing assets, if needed, because not everyone on their marketing team had the time or skill set to translate messaging into different copy.

My clients proved that messaging can be both clear enough to guide copy *and* engaging enough to be used directly in marketing, if needed. Also, adding interest and personality to your messaging is a surefire way to get out of jargon territory.

Headlines are a great place to start because they capture your buyers' attention and draw them into your message. Here are three techniques.

### Evoke Emotion

Make your readers actually feel something by connecting to their past experiences. This approach will make your headline stand out in a crowd of rational, emotionless B2B tech headlines. To do this, reflect your customers' real pains and desires to jog their memory and remind them how it feels—because emotion gets attention and motivates people to make a change.

Before: Save time with fewer meetings.

After: Free yourself from back-to-back meetings.

### Swap in the Unexpected

Take your vanilla headline and swap out a regular word with an unexpected alternative. This is one of my favorite techniques because it's so easy and effective. For example, swap "repetitive" with "boring," or "excellence" with "awesomeness." These add personality and humanness to your writing. They also get your readers' attention by disrupting their eye while scanning the page.

Before: Brainstorm ideas together.

After: Riff on ideas together.

### Try Rhyming, Repetition, and Alliteration

Finally, three things you learned in school that you get to keep! Add a rhyme in your headline to give it a sing-songy element. Or use a repeating structure to add emphasis. Or challenge yourself to repeat first letters with alliteration. These classic writing techniques make your message roll off the tongue with a pleasing sound your brain can remember. (That's why so many slogans and jingles use them.)

Rhyming: Delete every spreadsheet.

Repetition: Helpful agents, happy customers.

Alliteration: Catch customer concerns.

Once you've spiced up your headline, here are four techniques to add some zest to the body of your messaging.

## Paint a Picture

Sometimes you have to use more—not fewer—words to make your message clear. And that's OK. Clear and concise writing isn't about compressing big ideas into one or two words.

That's how we end up with fuzzy, abstract phrases, like "outcome-based strategies" or "process transformation." These phrases are impossible to picture in your mind and hard to grasp.

Concrete messages often need a few extra words. For example, instead of saying "tool consolidation" you might say "no more juggling multiple tools." Instead of "all-in-one" you might say "everything you need at your fingertips." See how more words make things more clear?

Concrete examples make your reader light up in an "oh, I see what you mean" kinda way.

And that lightbulb moment is totally worth the word count.

So get specific. Show benefits in the context of your readers' life. Describe what it actually looks like through their lens. It should be something they can picture in their mind.

Before: Improve customer communication and payment.

After: End games of phone tag and make it easy for customers to pay with built-in email, texting, and payment options.

### Show the Pro without the Con

Show how your customers can achieve something positive without the shortcomings of their current way of doing things. The goal is to remind your readers of their current problem and add an emotional response by calling it out. This works in headlines and body copy equally well, using one key word: *without*. As in, "It helps you do X without the Y."

Examples:

* Know where your project stands *without* having to call a status meeting.

* Find what you need *without* searching across tools.

* Understand user behavior *without* drowning in the numbers.

### Mix Up the Pace

Vary the length of your sentences to add momentum and oomph. If you have a long sentence, follow it up with a short one. Like this. This helps draw the reader through.

Before: Get visibility into your current shipping operations and relevant insights into future costs and expenditures. The right software solution and the right experts will save your business time and money.

After: See where your shipping costs are today—and where they'll be tomorrow—in a snap. No more surprises.

### Drop Some Parentheses

Emphasize a point and connect with readers using occasional parentheses. Brackets catch the eye because they're a disruption when you're scanning that tell you, "There's something important here!" Plus, they're a fun and playful way to show your brand's personality and make it clear there's a human on the other side of the message. Parentheses give the vibe of a friend whispering an aside in your ear (as though you're getting the inside scoop—like this). It gives you permission to almost break away from the "writing" and keep it real.

Example:

Stop looking for a needle in the haystack of online leads. Make people feel special with personalized campaigns (and prove you're an actual human) so you get more responses, applications, and appointments.

## Messaging in Translation

Can you spice up your messaging if it's going to be translated into different languages? You absolutely can—as long as you avoid using colloquialisms (e.g., "nip issues in the bud") that don't translate. Always aim for simple and concise language. Shorter words and sentences will set your messaging up to be clearly translated for global audiences.

# A PUNCHY PEP TALK

In Punchy Training Workshops, marketers spend several hours writing and refining a few ultra-clear and compelling messages. At the end, everyone is like, "Wow! I forgot how long it takes to write really good messaging."

And it's true—many people forget (or don't know) that crafting messaging that stands out and connects with your audience takes time. Amazon and Netflix have conditioned us to demand things instantly. We don't want to wait. And in B2B tech, things are always moving at breakneck speed.

However, writing is more than slapping words on a page. It's a form of thinking. You sharpen your thoughts and ideas through the writing process and, at the end, you have clarity that simply wasn't there before.

That clarity is critical to building a winning perception in the market. Give yourself the time and space to put all you've got into your messaging.

# 10

## *PAINT A PICTURE*

**Translate your messaging into a story that connects**

**W**HENEVER I create messaging for clients, I include a punchy story that brings the value proposition and benefits of the company or product to life. That way when you read it, you grasp the big picture behind the messaging and connect deeply with the customer's challenges and aspirations.

I've seen these stories bring humanity and emotions to the foreground of even the most technical products, like when I presented the story for a high-tech company that designed and manufactured a tiny-yet-critical component for a visionary product. The story showed how they were helping customers solve critical sustainability challenges. By the end, their CRO had to grab a tissue to wipe his eyes. Sure, maybe he was having a bad day, but I like to believe it's the power of story that moved him to tears.

Much has been written about the science of storytelling, but my favorite fact is that your brain thinks stories are real. When you read a book or watch a movie, your mind automatically places you inside the action. You feel as if the hero's reality is your reality.

We can't help but get emotionally invested in a story. That's why we hang on every word of a friend's juicy gossip about that weird neighbor. Or feel pissed off when a movie ends without giving us the resolution we need. Or cry when a beloved character dies. Stories make us care.

You can use this to your advantage by turning your messaging into a story where your customer is the hero and has big-picture context for your value proposition and benefits. So whoever reads it will see themselves in the story—and feel the urgency and emotion behind the messaging.

But not every type of messaging needs a story. Use this exercise when you're messaging something big and important, like your company or a major product release. The story would appear on key webpages, like the Why Us? page; shape the beginning of your first call deck; and inspire corporate videos, talks, and other campaigns.

There's a functional bonus too: a story gives colleagues and external partners a clearer, richer understanding of your messaging. They can read it once and get the full picture of the challenges your customer is facing, how your product can help, and why it all matters. And this will help them create effective sales and marketing materials that align with your message.

## The Punchy Story Framework

The Punchy Story Framework is inspired by the concept of the hero's journey from Joseph Campbell's book *The Hero with a Thousand Faces*. It's a twelve-stage plot structure that appears in many classic myths and stories, from *Beowulf* to *Harry Potter*. It outlines the familiar story of a hero going on an adventure that ultimately changes them for good. You just have to remember that your technology is not the hero of your story. That honor belongs to your customer.

The full hero's journey works great for Hollywood trilogies, but we want to keep our story punchy. So here are five simple phases to tell yours:

1 The Shift
2 The Villain
3 Three Obstacles
4 The Dream
5 The Solution

**Phase 1: The Shift**

Your story begins with a shift in your customer's world that forces them to make a change. In *Star Wars*, the shift for Luke Skywalker was finding out the Empire blew up his childhood home—an act of evil that forces him to go on a quest to fight the Empire. The thing about shifts is that they can't be ignored—your customer has no choice but to respond.

The shift in your story can be small or big—as long as it's meaningful and recognizable to your customer. Ideally, it's something they can relate to and are already feeling the need to change. Examples of shifts could be:

- A global trend, like the shift to remote work or changing consumer expectations

- A change in how things are done, like moving to the cloud or digitization

- An internal change, like more pressure on your team or seeking more purpose in work

Let's use Slack, circa 2014, as an example. The shift happening was that tech-focused teams were collaborating digitally and moving faster than ever before, but their current mode of communication couldn't keep pace.

This shift is super relatable for pretty much anyone working on a team or company, trying to communicate to get stuff done. And it kicks off our story in the right arena of work and productivity.

### Phase 2: The Villain

Every story has a villain—without them, there'd be no conflict, tension, or resolution at the end. The story would be flat and dull. Villains are great for stories because they put a face on a central problem the hero is facing. This makes it easy for the reader or viewer to get behind the hero's quest to defeat them. We see Darth Vader in all his evilness and shake our fists in the air, rooting even harder for Luke to win.

In your story, the villain emerges from the shift that's happening to your customer. This villain puts a face on the core problem your product is solving and is likely connected to your one big win. It's important that the villain is something distinct that you can name. Examples are:

- An object, like a spreadsheet or sticky notes
- An approach, like using point solutions as temporary bandages
- A concept, like blind spots in your customer service or complexity
- A person, like a hacker

Slack famously named the villain to be email. Old-fashioned email was getting in the way of productivity because it took too long for people to respond, things got lost in threads, and you could never find things fast enough in your inbox. Email is a great villain because many people could relate to its problems—and these were the people most likely to enjoy Slack. Sometimes the villain isn't universal, but it should be applicable to your A+ customer.

**Phase 3: Three Obstacles**
The villain tries to thwart the hero by throwing obstacles in their path. Darth Vader used Stormtroopers and fighter planes to try to stop Luke. And your villain is putting obstacles in front of your customer, too. The obstacles are concrete, distinct subproblems that trickle from the bigger problem.

Name the three main obstacles created by your villain. And yes, I'm asking you to do three again, not because I'm obsessed with the number, but because these obstacles should map to the pains covered in your three benefits and add context to them. Examples of obstacles might be:

- Objects and things, like non-stop alerts
- Daily occurrences, like breakdowns in manual processes
- Emotions, like feeling unsure or lacking confidence in something

Back to Slack—the three obstacles created by email were:

1 Can't find what you need to get work done (maps to Slack's benefit of being able to search and find anything quickly)

2   Missing out on stuff with siloed communication (maps to Slack's benefit of having organized group conversations)

3   Replies are taking too long (maps to Slack's benefit of messaging that's faster than email)

See how these obstacles show why the hero can't live with the villain? They illustrate the subproblems your customer has to deal with and connect to the benefits your product offers.

### Phase 4: The Dream

Dreams are what inspire and motivate us to overcome challenges—we all have them. The dream is how your customer wishes things would be, if only that darn villain and his obstacles weren't getting in the way. In *Star Wars*, Luke Skywalker dreamed of peace in the galaxy—that's what got him out of bed each morning. Break down the dream into two parts:

- The tangible thing or outcome customers want—for example, 24/7 threat protection they can count on
- How they'll feel when it happens—peace of mind

The truth is, we often desire "things" but what we really want is the feeling we think we'll have once that thing is in our possession. That's why I like to bring both into the story. For example, your customer may say they want to automate boring, manual tasks. But really, they want to make a bigger, more strategic contribution to the business.

For Slack, the customer dreams of being more productive—without wasting time on admin and other busywork.

**Phase 5: The Solution**

This is where your product finally enters the story to provide a helping hand. Luke Skywalker's solution was the Force, which he used to overcome the obstacles and defeat Darth Vader so he could achieve his dream of peace in the galaxy. Note how the Force was a tool, but not the thing that defeated the villain—it was Luke, backed by the superpower of the Force, who got the job done.

You want to think the same way. This is not where your software rides in on a trusty steed to save the day. Rather, your software is the magic weapon they need to overcome it all. This section is where you connect the dots between your unique delivery and the dream. It highlights the value proposition and three benefits and ends with the dream.

For example, Slack's solution was about making work simpler, more pleasant, and more productive by bringing together all of your team's communication in one place with real-time messaging, archive, and search.

See how it's high level? You don't want to start going into all the features and how it works—just show how the benefits and value proposition map to the villain and obstacles that you set up before.

## How to Craft Your Story Paragraph by Paragraph

Once you've gone through the exercise and brought all the pieces together, write a brief, four-paragraph story. I've read some narratives that go on and on forever. But we're not going to do that. Just like everything else, I want you to make it punchy—so the story is clear.

Remember, paragraph one sets up the shift, two introduces the villain and obstacles, three connects to the customer's dream, and four presents your solution.

The most important thing is to make sure the story resonates with people. At Punchy, we write the story from the customer's perspective, using the second-person "you"—as if the story is directly addressing the customer. This helps it feel more immediate and human. But you can easily write it from the third-person perspective if that feels more appropriate to you.

Here's an example based on a fictional AI chatbot for customer support, named Chatty. The hero of the story is the head of customer experience.

### Paragraph 1: Set Up the Shift

In the opening paragraph, you state the shift your customer is facing and how it's directly affecting them. Beware of spending too long on the preamble and the state of the world—you want to quickly connect the dots between the macro shift in the world and how it's showing up in your customer's life. Aim to make this paragraph no more than three sentences long.

The shift Chatty's customer is facing is how modern consumers expect to interact with brands. Brands used to dictate when and where customers could get in touch with questions, and for support. Now, consumers hold the power and demand instant support on their channel of choice—or else they'll take their issue to social media.

Example: *Today's customers come at you from every angle 24/7—they're on every channel, and they want answers and help now (like, now now).*

# Choose a villain
## that everyone can get behind

**Paragraph 2: Introduce the Villain and the Obstacles**

In the second paragraph, you introduce the story's villain and the three obstacles. Remember, the goal is to connect to un-ignorable problems that your customer will recognize and relate to. This is where you describe problems in the context of your customer's life. Aim to make this paragraph no more than five sentences.

The villain Chatty's customer is facing is a growing mountain of support desk tickets. This is a tangible thing—it's also the highest motivating pain for prospects, the reason they start looking for a solution in the first place.

The obstacles these support tickets cause are:

1 Existing team is overworked and having to focus on low-value work

2 Constantly having to hire and onboard new reps to try to keep up

3 Risk to brand reputation damage

Example: *But your customer support team can't be everywhere, solving every issue. And they don't want to either—who likes answering the exact same question two hundred times a day? Your team is built to handle your customers' toughest problems, not track a package or find a knowledge base article. But you can't hire and train enough live agents to keep up with all the questions—and keep the social media trolls at bay.*

**Paragraph 3: Connect to Your Customer's Dream**

The third paragraph is where you introduce your customer's dream and how they wish things were going differently.

This dream brings the emotional side to your benefits. Aim to write no more than three sentences.

The dream of Chatty's customer is to make sure every one of their customers gets the right resolution as quickly as possible—ideally, without always having to talk to the support team. That way, their support team can focus their time on the customer requests that need their expertise.

Example: *You want to help customers find answers fast and walk away with a smile. You want your team engaged when real expertise is the only way to get the job done. You need a way to make your support team's job easier, not harder.*

### Paragraph 4: Present Your Solution

The fourth paragraph is where you finally get to present your product as the solution to the customer's problems and the answer to their dream. Introduce the value proposition and three benefits, and end it with a nod to why it matters in the big picture.

Note that you don't go into features or how it works here—you want to write just enough to clarify what your solution is and what it can do.

Chatty's value proposition is the ability to provide the kind of support the customers want with their existing team. And the benefits are (1) provide immediate 24/7 support, (2) free up agents to be more strategic, and (3) provide a better customer experience.

Example: *Provide the modern customer support your consumers demand with Chatty's customer support bot. It engages your customers so seamlessly they won't miss a human agent, but it's ready to find one if someone needs it. Customers leave with the answers they need and a great impression of your brand. With Chatty, you can give your customers a conversation that really says something.*

Once you've written the story out, the following are some clarifying questions to ask yourself, based on common issues my clients have had with this exercise.

**Are your customers aware of the villain and obstacles?** You want them to be obvious and undeniable to your customer. These have to be things your customer has already identified as issues. One thing that happens a lot is that you see an underlying problem that isn't clear to your customer. Like we've talked about before, you want to meet your customers where they're at and frame the problems as they see them.

**Does your villain potentially offend someone?** Sometimes people mistake the villain for someone who is doing something negative. For example, I once had a client who cited their own sales team as the villain! While I saw where they were coming from, I advised them to choose a villain that would unite their organization rather than divide it. So, choose a villain that everyone can get behind, like a giant Excel spreadsheet.

**Is the shift too big, vague, and/or a cliché?** I can't tell you how many stories I've heard that start with "the world has changed"—that's a no-brainer. When it comes to innovation and tech the world is constantly changing. It's fine if you want to start there when you brainstorm but keep going. Then reread what you wrote and see if you can start later in the story. The key is to make it very connected to your customer and their awareness.

Does your solution paragraph dive into the technical weeds? You can't start a story that talks about your customers' feelings and challenges, and then dive straight into machine learning models and real-time analytics in the next paragraph. It's too big a leap. Remember the goal of a story is to grasp the high-level messaging.

## Using the Punchy Story Framework to Refine or Kickstart Your Messaging

Sometimes, doing this story exercise will bring up new angles and ideas to improve your messaging framework draft. For example, I was working with a company in the email security space. Their platform helped businesses protect their email from sophisticated attacks, with a behavioral engine and through an AI-bot that told employees whether a certain email was safe to open or not.

In the messaging framework, we focused on the platform's ability to stop the hardest attacks—the impersonation attack. But when we did the story exercise, we realized the main villain wasn't the hacker sending these threats—that was too big. The villain was traditional user training courses that told employees what to do when they got a suspicious email. These once-a-year training sessions weren't enough to teach employees what to do, which is why breaches continued to happen from users opening emails they shouldn't.

We realized this was a unique and tangible villain— something we could really tackle, unlike all the bad hackers in the world. We originally had this idea as a benefit, but we decided to elevate it into the value proposition because it was so tied to their differentiation in the market. And this helped the platform stand out from other solutions who relied too heavily on bragging about their "market-leading" tech.

This story exercise can also help you get started with drafting your messaging as it gives you another way to frame your thinking.

## A PUNCHY PEP TALK

In my experience, this is the easiest (and most fun) exercise in the entire book. And it's a great opportunity to get a wider group involved—because all humans are wired for stories, not just marketers and creatives. Have fun with this one! Picture each phase of the story like a blockbuster movie. Imagine what the scenes look like for your customer, from facing the villain to tackling the obstacles. Amp up the drama! Even if the brainstorm goes nowhere, spending time imagining life as your customer is a worthwhile exercise.

# PART THREE

# IMPLEMENTATION

Launch your messaging with success. In this section,
you'll learn how to validate your new messaging, apply it
to sales and marketing assets, and get your colleagues
on board—so you can tell a consistent story to the market.

# 11

# *PUT IT OUT THERE*

**Launch your messaging into the world**

**C**ONGRATULATIONS! You've made it to the end and finally finished writing your new messaging. So far, you've learned to connect with your customers' pains and desires, highlight your product's unique difference, and craft a clear and compelling value proposition and benefits. Pat yourself on the back for doing all that hard work...

...then get ready to do a bit more. Because now that the writing is done, it's time to put it into action. This final stage dictates the true success of your new messaging. And it all hinges on getting other people in your company to consistently use your messaging—which is a whole other kind of challenge.

There are zillions of messaging documents gathering dust on drives around the world, filed and forgotten. Some never even got off the ground. The two most common reasons this happens are:

1  The messaging document is too complicated and hard to use. In other words, it's pointless. So people make up their own messaging.

2  Stakeholders aren't aligned on the new messaging. Sales thinks one thing, marketing thinks another, and

the CEO has a totally different idea. Without alignment, everyone just sticks with whatever they've been using.

Luckily, you've avoided the first problem by writing punchy messaging. Now let's tackle the second one: how to get everyone using it.

## Get Buy-In and Alignment for Your New Messaging

I may call myself a messaging strategist, but I'm really more of an alignment strategist when I consult with teams (if you know, you know). Alignment is as important as it is hard to achieve. What I've learned is that the less involved others are in the overall process, the less likely your messaging will get used by people. When someone tosses a new messaging document over the fence, it can feel like a "take it or leave it" kinda thing. Some may use it, while others will stick with what they've got. And this leads to inconsistent messaging that confuses your audience and market. But when you're part of the process, you naturally feel like you're part of the solution.

That's why I recommend an inclusive approach that involves key stakeholders in your messaging process. It may seem like extra up-front work, but I promise you that it's the fastest way to get alignment and buy-in. Hands down.

## Get Your Cross-Functional Messaging Gang Together

Gather up a cross-functional team that represents different perspectives on the business, especially one that is particularly close to your buyers and existing customers. For big messaging initiatives—for example, for your company or a major product release—I'll typically pull together the heads of marketing, sales, product, and customer success, as well as the CEO. Plus, I like to include additional salespeople who are close to the customer. Try to keep the group as tight as possible (a maximum of twelve people is fine, but fewer if you can).

For smaller messaging initiatives—like a new feature or solution—it's enough to bring in one or two people who are close to the product and customer, like a product manager and someone from sales. Your working group could be as small as three people. If there's someone who's critical for buy-in but doesn't have the time to join your team, then make sure you incorporate their input.

## Go Through the Punchy Messaging Process Together

I once worked with a popular sales tech platform that had a cross-functional team of fifteen *big* personalities. To be honest, I wondered if I'd be able to pull off the alignment with them. Everyone on that team had their own strong opinion about what made their platform special, and what buyers needed to hear about. What became clear is that while everyone had a lot of knowledge in their head about the product, the market, their buyers, etc.—none of them really understood what messaging was or how to go about doing it. My process gave them a clear framework (with guardrails) to share their knowledge and ideas. And it forced the conversations to be productive.

The exercises generated discussion and made the team address issues they didn't even realize they had. For example, they knew exactly who was in their buying group, but they hadn't ever gotten more specific. As a result we changed their A+ customer to one who had more sway with budgets. We also got even more clear on their customer pains. With so many salespeople in the room, they knew *exactly* what customers cared about, what benefits made their eyes light up, and what they were interested in. It reminded me how all the necessary knowledge is often right inside your organization—you just need a way to extract it. We hashed it all out and eventually presented new messaging that was built on real customer knowledge, their product's magic, and a group effort.

I had minimal revisions to make when the CMO pinged me and said with disbelief, "People in the company are already using the new messaging. I can't believe it." She was a veteran CMO who'd run many messaging initiatives at large companies. And she was prepared to work hard to get everyone in her org to use the new messaging. Instead, she was already hearing echoes of the new value proposition and benefits in customer success and sales—without even formally "operationalizing" the new messaging. Heck, it wasn't even finalized yet.

"They're using it almost by osmosis," she said.

It was organically spreading through the organization because customer success and sales had been part of the process, and naturally felt like part of the solution. They understood where it came from, and how to use it. The working sessions proved to be buy-in sessions, and they couldn't wait to get everyone using it.

*That* is the power of an inclusive approach, where everyone contributes.

Take your team through the Punchy Messaging Process in this book. But use this cheat: go through the process alone first, then have your recommendations handy when you take the rest of the team through it. This gives you time and space to come to a good working draft, while leaving room for others to contribute their ideas. As a consultant, I do the heavy lifting of research and strategy before the meetings and focus our time together to make decisions and get aligned. That way, busy colleagues can make their contributions in a few hours, rather than be dragged out across several weeks.

Just know that you will get feedback and have to manage revisions no matter what. There's no way of avoiding it. I don't know what it is about words that makes everyone have an opinion—but not all opinions are equal. Stick to the writing formulas and techniques in this book and go for real, human language. Watch out for any feedback that goes against the previously aligned and agreed-upon strategy from the sessions. If you see it, let them know that what they're suggesting would require a strategy change.

## Three Common Alignment Obstacles (and How to Overcome Them)

Alignment is one of the biggest challenges in business, and if you've tried to get aligned before, you know how tricky it can be. After running more than a hundred messaging engagements with cross-functional teams at tech companies of all sizes and at all stages, I have seen hiccups of every kind popping up—here are some of the most common ones, and how you can navigate them.

### 1. Not Everyone Understands What a Messaging Strategy Is or How It's Used

I've been guilty of assuming that everyone in the room knows what messaging is and how it fits in the big picture.

But this is rarely the case for people beyond the marketing team. When people aren't sure what's involved in a messaging strategy and how it fits in the big picture, they don't really know what they're working on, and that can lead to a lot of confusion. Avoid this by clearly defining messaging and how it relates to positioning and content at the beginning, so everyone starts on the same page. (You can reference this book's introduction for help with that.) Be prepared to educate along the way where needed.

## 2. Getting Too Wrapped Up in What Competitors Are Saying

Curiosity about what others are doing can help you stand out, but if you go too far and obsess over every campaign your competition runs or every word they use, you'll get derailed. (Remember that messaging engagement I told you about where the CEO asked if they could still use the word "growth" because their direct competitor was using it in a headline?) If conversation keeps drifting toward what other companies are doing, remind people to stay focused on your product and your customers. Own your product's unique value and resist the urge to react or emulate what other companies are doing.

## 3. Fear-Based Decisions

Fear of leaving something out. Fear of not sounding innovative enough. Fear that the CEO won't like it. When fear drives decisions, they usually aren't the right ones. If you sense an undercurrent of fear or worry about something, name it and talk about it. Have faith in your company, vision, and customers. You can also build confidence with customer research and feedback.

**It takes a clear message repeated again and again (and again) to build a winning perception**

Remember, the more open and honest everyone is, the better it will go. And your messaging will have a better chance of success in the real world.

## How to Build Confidence in Your New Messaging

The tech industry is all about testing and validation. People often ask me how to validate whether their messaging is right (or not) before launching.

I tell them there's no way to one hundred percent validate a messaging strategy before putting it out into the world. Messaging isn't copy on a landing page you can A/B test—it's a strategic story that guides marketing activities. The process for writing punchy messaging in this book is built on a firm understanding of your customer and simple, clear language, which stacks the cards in your favor. But like a new positioning strategy, it must be put into action to get real feedback from customers and the market.

You can build confidence in your new messaging by getting some of that feedback early on. Here are three simple ways to validate your messaging and gather up enough courage to launch.

### 1. Have Sales Test-Drive It in Calls and Outbound Emails

Human reactions are my favorite kind of data. And salespeople are running their own messaging tests with prospects all day! They have their finger on the pulse of what's working and what's not. So, ask a few trusted sellers to float your messaging in prospect calls. Have them gauge how people are reacting. Are they nodding along? Are their eyes lighting up? This is a fast way to get a gut feeling for how well the messaging is landing.

### 2. Run Your Messaging by Existing Customers

If you have relationships with customers, consider bringing a few together in a focus group or having the messaging vetted by user groups. In my experience, they'll be particularly good at recommending whether certain phrases and words will resonate with your customer or not.

### 3. Share Your Messaging with Analysts

If you have relationships with analysts, you can run your messaging by them and ask for their thoughts. Analysts have a good perspective on the market and how other solutions are messaging themselves. However, it's important to remember that analysts—while very knowledgeable—aren't your customer; they can't say for sure how it will land with your buyers.

Launching new messaging requires a leap of faith to some extent. You just have to put your best foot forward with the resources available to you. If you're at an earlier stage company, you might not have a bunch of customers to speak to. If you're at a product-led company, you might not have a sales team who can try out your messaging. Just do the best you can with whatever you've got to work with.

Put your messaging out there and give it a few months to get an accurate read on how it's being received. Resist the temptation to switch gears too soon. Otherwise, you'll confuse people and muddy your testing.

## How to Roll Out Your Messaging across the Organization

Once everyone is on the same page and feeling confident about the messaging, it's time to infuse it into your sales and marketing materials and to empower your colleagues to use it. Here are the tactical steps for executing new messaging across your company.

### Update Your Website

The website is your first stop for updating new messaging. Company messaging should guide the content on the homepage, and product messaging should live on the relevant webpage, like a product page for example. The value proposition informs the hero marquee at the top of the page, and the benefits come next. Any existing social proof, case studies, and highlighted features can remain as they are. But look for opportunities to infuse your unique difference and value proposition into your crossheads. For example, if your value proposition is about "helping teams work together, faster" you could update the headline above your customer success stories to say: "Hear from top teams working at top speed."

For new company messaging, update the beginning of your About or Company page to reflect your story. Keep it focused on the customer, so they can connect with the full context of your messaging. Typical About pages are where companies talk about themselves. But it's far more interesting to the readers if you lead with the story about the villain and obstacles they're facing, and how your company can help them achieve their dream. Most clients I've worked with simply put their punchy story on the About page. Your company history, timeline, investors, and stats can follow this story further down the page.

### Update First Call Deck and Sales Enablement

For new company or platform messaging, update the beginning of your first call deck to reflect your story. Each slide represents a stage of the story.

Slide 1: Introduce the shift that's happening to your buyer

Slide 2: Name the villain

Slide 3: Set up the three obstacles your buyer is facing

Slide 4: Mirror the dream—the way your buyer wishes things could be

Slide 5: Introduce your company/product with the value proposition

Slides 6–8: Expand on one benefit per slide

From slide 9 onward, you can keep your existing slides on results, customer stories, and other social proof.

The challenge is summing up each stage of the story in one headline per slide. Keep each slide ruthlessly focused on the Single Most Important Takeaway (SMIT). Update any other partner or sales enablement pieces—like one-sheeters and shorter decks—to reflect new messaging.

### Update Bios and Boilerplates

For company messaging, you'll need to update your PR boilerplate, company description, and wherever your bio appears on socials, Google, directories, etc. Remember that prospects are finding your company through many different channels, and an outdated bio could be a missed opportunity to catch someone's interest.

To write your boilerplate, start with the last paragraph of your punchy story. In the first sentence, clarify what your product is and introduce the value proposition. Next, touch on each of the three benefits, add customer validation, and end it with a nod to why it matters in the big picture.

Note that you don't go into features or how it works here—you want to include just enough to clarify what your solution is and what it can do.

Here's an example for Chatty (the made-up company) from the last chapter:

*Chatty is an AI customer support platform that delivers the speedy, modern help experience consumers want. With automation and a friendly chatbot, Chatty delivers fast resolutions for customers and gives support teams insights into opportunities to improve their products and services. It makes sure every customer gets the personal service and expert answers they expect, and it's simple for agents to use. Trusted by leading brands like Vimeo, Under Armour, and Ring, Chatty delivers a brand-boosting experience that lightens the load for support teams.*

### Evolve Content Strategy and Customer Stories

This is more long term, but you'll want your content strategy to mirror your new messaging, so you're educating the market on the problems you solve. Each benefit area could connect to a content pillar, where you create content for different stages of the funnel on that topic. Your content team and any freelancers you work with will love having a concrete message to work with that they can infuse into your company's content. The unique value you've established for your product or company will help them create content that stands out from your competitors.

If your value proposition has changed a lot, consider getting new customer case studies that highlight that result. It's likely already happening—your messaging is built on that value you're offering—but case studies might not be written that way. For the example of "helping teams work together, faster" you could write new case studies that clarify the speed and results. So you're eventually building up customer stories that support your new messaging.

### Launch Your Messaging Internally to Create a Buzz

Don't just Slack people with a link to the new company messaging document—get people on board with a share-out. Some of the most successful messaging engagements I've ever done included a company all-hands where we shared the journey of the process, presented the messaging, and answered people's questions. This is a great way to get buy-in and involvement for the new messaging.

You could also hold several working sessions where people from different teams get tips on how to infuse the new messaging into their work. For example, CS might want to know how to adjust onboarding emails, sales might want to adjust outbound emails, and the demand generation team might want to brainstorm running new campaigns.

Remember, the more involved people are in the messaging process, the more likely they are to use it. In my experience, everyone wants to feel like they're an important part of it—which they are!

### Know That Consistency Is Key

Once your messaging has gone public, see how it resonates. Positive responses from the sales team are one of the best early indicators of success.

Continue sending the same consistent message through sales and marketing activities, no matter how dull that consistency feels. You may feel like a broken record repeating the same thing, in a slightly different way, over and over. You might even assume that the market is as bored of it as you are and want to mix things up.

But here's the thing: just as you start getting bored of the message is about the same time the market finally starts hearing it. That could be six to twelve months from launch. It takes a clear message repeated again and again (and again) to build a winning perception in the market. If it's working, keep at it—and all your efforts will pay dividends.

# CONCLUSION

**T**HIS BOOK EXISTS because I wanted to answer all the messaging questions marketers, founders, and CEOs have asked me over the years. And I created these frameworks and techniques to tackle the real-world challenges of communicating the awesomeness of a tech product in fast-moving, crowded markets.

But every company has special challenges and considerations depending on your industry, product, target customer, market, and growth goals. That's what makes Punchy Training Workshops so effective. When marketers practice applying these techniques to their own products and companies, they get to address new questions as they spring up and go deep—like *really* deep—into the nuances of messaging.

I've tried to answer every last question you might have about messaging, but there will always be new ones that pop up, like:

- Is this the right value proposition, or not?
- Should I focus on X, Y, or Z in this benefit?
- Is this benefit too broad?
- Is "streamline" jargon?!

Since I won't be there to give you a specific answer (unless you join a Punchy Training Workshop, of course!), I'll leave you with this final piece of advice: always champion your customer. I know, I know—I've been saying this throughout the whole dang book. But it bears repeating one last time because it's easy to lose sight of this truth when you're in the thick of writing messaging. It's easy to get wrapped up in all the information, stay stuck in your head, and keep overcomplicating things. Championing your customer is the simplest path to messaging success. So, if you're questioning what you've written, or unsure if you're going in the right direction, ask yourself: "Does this messaging make it easier for buyers to see how we can help them?"

That is the ultimate goal of messaging—to show your buyer how their life could improve with the support of your product, as quickly and effortlessly as possible. That's it. Move toward things that support this goal, and away from things that detract from it. This will help you cut the fluff and focus on what truly matters. Championing your customer is more than just an approach—it's putting good intentions behind your messaging. Buyers will pick up on that. They'll feel seen and heard, which sparks interest and trust in your company. Make it all about them, not your product, and trust you're headed in the right direction.

Here's to your messaging success—you've got this!

JACKIE BUTLER

# ABOUT THE AUTHOR

EMMA STRATTON is a messaging expert and founder of Punchy, a training and consulting firm that helps tech companies win hearts and minds through simple, human messaging. Since 2015, Emma has developed messaging strategies for leading companies like Loom, Outreach, Miro, and Uber. Marketers from around the world have trained with Emma to learn how to write punchy messaging, including teams at Salesforce, Atlassian, and Oracle. She lives in Portland, Oregon, with her husband and three kids.

# WORK WITH PUNCHY TO WRITE BETTER MESSAGING

Want to go further with the messaging techniques explored in this book? Emma and her team at Punchy offer several ways to make that happen.

### Punchy Messaging Training

Punchy offers live group training experiences that give marketing teams and individuals the theory and practice to create clear, compelling, and human messaging—every time. Emma's popular Punchy Messaging for B2B Tech course combines on-demand videos, hands-on workshops, and feedback sessions to help you up your messaging game. And for companies that want a comprehensive training program, Punchy also offers courses on positioning, copywriting, storytelling, and more.

### Consulting

Emma has consulted with hundreds of tech companies of all shapes and stages, from cybersecurity to sales tech. Today, she partners directly with executive teams at high-growth B2B companies to help them get clear on the right positioning and create a messaging strategy that supports it.

### Speaking

Emma is a popular keynote speaker with a knack for breaking down complex messaging issues into simple, actionable takeaways. Her high-energy talks are engaging and fun, and she likes to combine them with in-person workshops, fireside chats, and Q&A sessions.

Let's talk about how we can help you write punchy messaging through our workshops, consulting, and live keynotes. Get in touch at punchy.co.

linkedin.com/in/emma-stratton-punchy

Made in the USA
Las Vegas, NV
06 September 2024

94876352R00125